Feđa Štukan
BLANK

TRANSLATED FROM BOSNIAN BY
Ediba-Bakira Trbonja-Kapić

COPYEDITOR
Chris Dale

PROOFREADER
Joe Shooman

DTP
Boriša Gavrilović

FRONT COVER DESIGN BY
Feđa Štukan

PRINTED BY
Dobra knjiga, Sarajevo

Feđa Štukan

BLANK

Sarajevo, 2020

For Aya

THE END

When he was two or three years old, he set off on a trip with his mother on his first flight. The memory is still ever so vivid, as if it happened only this morning. They were standing in a long, snake shaped queue of people, between poles connected with red rope. Mother used one hand to put the bag on the X-ray machine and the other to squeeze his hand tighter, at the same time making a barely noticeable gesture with her head towards the escalator so his attention turned in that direction. He looked and first saw dark caps, then faces with dark sunglasses, then shoulders with yellow captain stripes on the epaulettes, three torsos with ties and behind them, four beautiful uniformed women. They were all at least a metre taller than him. He stood there, eyes wide open, completely mesmerised with the image. "Pilots and stewardesses", his mother whispered into his ear. The check-in staff took off the red rope connecting two poles, and with utmost respect and a wide hand gesture told the crew to skip the line and place their bags on the X-ray. The three men also with great respect and in an almost rehearsed motion, repeated the gesture to the girls to go in front of them, which they did, with wide, beautiful smiles, nodding their heads in sync. While waiting in turn the pilot with the most golden stripes looked down toward him, pushing his dark glasses down his nose a bit. He looked the boy in the eye and winked. That was the moment that changed the his life. At that very moment, he too became a pilot.

BLANK

"Sit down and write!", William Bradley told me on a penthouse terrace of the Roosevelt Hotel on Hollywood Boulevard.

"Write what?"

"Throw it all on paper and we'll make a film! It's interesting!"

"Maybe. Where should I start?"

"Here. Start from the top of this hotel and how you came to be here."

"How come I am in this job or in this hotel?"

"Whichever. Just write!"

The waitress came with a tray. William took the Jack with two ice cubes. I just had water due to my fucked up liver and pancreas.

* * *

BANG!

I placed the little cross of my sniper optics right upon the enemy's forehead and I pulled the trigger.

BANG!

He's done!

Yes, that's how it all started.

* * *

Even though shells constantly flew over our positions and landed somewhere in the city, this was one of the quieter frontlines. The quietest I had been to so far. We weren't attacking each other, at least not with infantry. It was an agreement made on a higher level. Separation lines were drawn years before so 'us' and 'them' were right where we should be. It was well known how badly armed we were: it was also ever so obvious by now. We hadn't responded to a single artillery attack; we had nothing to respond with due to the arms embargo. Still, they didn't overrun us with tanks, although they had a few there and they could have if they'd wanted to. Realistically, we couldn't stop them with one bazooka or the Russian Malyutka which we were saving for a rainy day and which none of us knew how to operate anyway. Random killing of civilians in the city was much more efficient, didn't take courage, carried no risk and yet was much more symbolic. My grandfather Milan, a strategy professor at the military academy, taught me a thing or two and not just me but he also taught all the educated generals of our army, including those across on the other side from us.

Shifts on our frontline were a week long and then we had two weeks off. We usually spent them resting in the city. But on that seventh day, the last day of the shift, our commander told us that our lines were to be attacked and ordered us to stay put until further notice. I remember the order struck me as a bad one, especially because I knew our counter-intelligence was clueless and that they wouldn't know when an attack would take place. Or rather they knew there *wouldn't* be one, but they had to pretend that they knew there *would* be, so that we appeared to be a serious army that had intelligence officers everywhere. This meant, that once more, we would spend another seven, ten or maybe twenty days ready and on the edge. And that in the end the attack wouldn't happen. Maybe that's why they were called counter-intelligence; because they gave information counter to what would actually happen. This really pissed me off.

I took my sniper rifle, went inside one of the ruins and waited. For hours. I thought I would just kill the first thing on their side that moved. My right eye swelled up from looking through the optics for so long. And then, finally, I saw the silhouette of a soldier on the top of the hill across from our position. Indigo blue sky behind him. I could even see him without the optics.

It was as if he was standing and pissing in our direction, or maybe he was just standing. The sun was setting and I couldn't tell exactly. Pissing or not, the opportunity was there to get a promotion commendation, medals and most importantly, relief from the frustration of our prolonged shift.

500 metres. I aligned the sights.

I placed the little cross of my sniper optics right on his forehead and pulled the trigger.

BANG!

He's done.

That's how it all started.

I was angry. A huge amount of adrenaline was literally buzzing through my body. I could clearly hear my own pulse. My heartbeat was making my body twitch so badly that I could barely get the rifle still to see the result of my shot through the optics.

"Fuck your Serb mother, it is because of you I have to be here for another fucking week," I muttered through my teeth.

I calmed the rifle and looked through the optics. He was still standing in his place. I quickly pulled the breech lever back, putting a new bullet in the barrel, adjusted the optics and BANG! A second bullet. Third, fourth, fifth, new magazine, sixth, seventh, eighth. I shot at his head, above his head, to the left and to the right. I shot at his legs. Yet, still nothing. Is it possible that I missed him so badly that he didn't even hear the bullets whizzing past? During our training we never shot at a target higher up than ourselves. It is the sniper that is usually higher than the target. This position calls for different calculation and sight settings. I was now out of ammo; eight bullets and that was it. If I was to get more ammo, I'd have to sneak through the trenches, to wriggle and crawl through the ruins, to turn over the whole armoury and a bunch of boxes hoping to find few bullets of that caliber, and by that time it was more likely that the Chetnik[1] would die a natural death than wait for me in the same spot so I could take him out. I gave up. I guess today was his lucky day.

* * *

The red sunset shines on me through the entrance to the trench. I manage to look at it with my eyes

---

1   Chetnik – Serbian nationalist para-military supported by the Orthodox Church. A century ago, Chetniks were the liberation guerrillas fighting the Ottomans in today's southern Serbia and Northern Macedonia; at the beginning of WW2, they were royalists, the so-called "King's army in the homeland" initially resisting the German occupation of Yugoslavia. However, their resistance turned into collaboration after they clashed with communist-led Tito's partisans, during which they committed atrocities against Bosnian Muslims and pro-Titoist local Serbs. The revival of the Chetnik rhetorics and paramilitary evoking the Chetniks of the past during the 1980s was simultaneous with the Serbian nationalism. Local nationalists; Muslims and Catholics use this term to denote all Orthodox Christians.

wide open. It's a discipline I try to perfect every evening, weather permitting. The amount of light entering the eye needs to be dosed by the eyelids. If too much light enters suddenly, it will blind you and you won't see the sunspots – small, barely visible black dots, and yet bigger than this whole shit hole called Planet Earth. The only thing in all of this we should be thankful for each day is this incredible, five-billion-year-old nuclear reaction whose dust we are made of; you, me and every one of those Chetniks out there. Each lump of lead, each grain of gunpowder, every chemical reaction in the brain, all love, fear and faith. Even this hatred we look at each other with through the sights was created by one such powerful speck on the edge of the rotating disc somewhere in the universe. I am sorry that for most it represents nothing more than something to tan the skin for a more exotic look.

From this admiring view I always fall deep in thought. Luckily, it lasts about two and a half minutes and unfortunately, such deep thought with its genius conclusion is usually pushed behind the horizon along with the last visible soft glowing rays.

I devote that sunset to the man I nearly killed. Who was he? Where was he from? What did he do before we became stupid? Did he have better things to do? He too had a photo album with pictures of him learning to walk, swim, wearing a rubber ring and armbands, a snorkelling mask and flippers. A photo of him going to school wearing a school rucksack with a 'Formula One' logo on it. A photo with an alphabet book. A photo with the whole class: he's cheerful and chubby, first in the top row on the right.

He got his first F in fifth grade, lit his first cigarette, was caught by his old man and beaten. He figured out jerking off, beer, then a joint. He learned three chords on a guitar so he could play 'Balkane moj' (My Balkans) at the beach in Zaostrog and lose his virginity to some falsely impressionable yet experienced Czech girl, who had no idea nor cared what the song was all about anyway.

Or maybe he hadn't had any of that? Maybe he couldn't swim, had never had a joint, never lost his virginity. Whatever, he probably had someone who loved him and was waiting for him, the same way they were waiting for me and hoping I would come back this time too. Alive and in one piece.

Someone would have knocked on his door tonight, with fake pride and a sad face, using a tried and tested tone of voice to say their son, father or brother has bravely and selflessly given his life in a heroic battle for Republika Srpska[2], and that he

---

2   At the beginning of 1990s, "Republika Srpska" was a para-state, founded on the expansionist idea of great Serbia, fully supported by the Republic of Serbia. After the signing of the Dayton Peace Agreement that stopped the war, BiH was divided into two entities. One of them, called Federation of BiH, covers the

would never be forgotten. The family would have been lost. Their lives would become such shit they would wish they were dead too. The next day, they would need to buy a coffin, to pay for transport, the priest, graveyard slot, print the obituaries and inform their relatives. Meanwhile, their souls would be breaking into atoms and all sense would be lost.

They would still gather on anniversaries, light candles, tell stories of events from his youth a thousand times over, trying to laugh to light up the atmosphere but finishing up by wiping their eyes with sodden handkerchiefs. And all that because he had to bravely and selflessly take a piss at the time I was pissed off.

I imagined my family in that position.

* * *

It's a millimetre to sunset.

* * *

"Why are you taking it to heart so much?", Comrade Sanin asked me while he was finishing rolling up

---

territory with the majority of Catholic and Muslim population, whilst the entity Republika Srpska has a majority Orthodox Christians population and encompasses 49% of the territory. During the war in the 1990s, that territory was thoroughly ethnically cleansed by pogrom and forceful displacement of Catholics and Muslims. Republika Srpska today still has the aspiration of secession from BiH and joining the Republic of Serbia.

a joint on a wooden ammo crate. "He would have taken you out in a second and wouldn't have given a fuck".

"It's just bad bro!"

"Fuck that and take this!", he said in a hoarse voice, puffing out smoke.

"I grew it myself", he boasted, "Don't tell the others we've got some, they'll smoke it all."

The two of us went through SWAT training together. The training was a top military and state secret. We were the best in our class.

Often when we got high (which was any time we were in the trench together and that was very often) we looked back on our training days. We remembered how while ninety of us SWAT trainees laid on our backs with our eyes closed, instructors ran over our stomachs, jumping from one to another. That drill could go on for hours. Our abs had to be tight throughout and we were not allowed to make a sound.

The punishment for any disobedience was 300 push-ups on grainy concrete with the palms up. If you couldn't endure it brutal force was used. Some guys would cry with joy if their wrists broke as that would mean the end of training.

"More blood in training, less in combat!", the instructors frequently repeated.

They taught us how to shoot any and every weapon; how to make bombs and how to jump out of cars and trucks at full speed onto concrete. I tore all my ligaments doing that. I could barely walk from the pain but I wasn't spared. They taught us to kill people with various different items and also without using such things. They taught us martial arts. They also taught us where to hide drugs and explosives in a car. They boasted how they once smuggled four tons of heroin across some border in a generator and when they were finally caught, they then killed all their captors. These stories made them laugh, hysterically and pleasurably. Talk about killing living creatures was hilarious to them.

Our morning class started with Qur'an recitals, and ended the same way. After each karate kick we had to shout "Allahu Akbar!", which was somewhat understandable since our instructors were Mujaheddin. Although politicians from my side will deny it until the day they die, the Mujaheddin did indeed train part of the regular BiH[3] Army.

Our final exam in tactics was to go into a real enemy building and 'clean it', by which I mean to kill anyone inside, regardless of their gender or age. The building that the group I led into happened to be empty. We broke the record though, we 'cleaned' the four storey building in one minute and forty-five seconds. Twenty of us.

---

3   BiH – 'Bosna i Hercegovina' or the Republic of Bosnia and Herzegovina – one of the six republics that made socialist Yugoslavia.

The practical part of the final explosives exam was to go out into an enemy minefield in the black of night and to dig out three mines each. Abaz taught the explosives.

At one of the lessons he showed us how to disable the MURD anti-personnel mine which explodes when you lift your leg off the firing pin. You push your bayonet (if you have it with you) at an angle between the firing pin and the sole of your shoe, then as deep as possible into the ground. Then you hold your comrade's hand (assuming he'll agree to that and risk losing his own limbs or life) he then pulls you as far and as fast from the mine as possible. That is the only option and usually an unsuccessful one. While Abaz was squatting down, holding a training mine between his legs, he asked for someone to pass him a knife so he could show how it is done. I'm not sure why, but at that moment I took my blade out of its sheath and from distance of four to five metres, threw it sticking it in the floor between the mine, his legs and his testicles. Everyone was left speechless. I thought he would send it back straight back and into my throat. Instead, all three instructors congratulated me with lunatic smiles and sparkles in their eyes, thumbs up on both hands. From then on, even though I sometimes shirked, I never did any push-ups as punishment. I was privileged as far as they were concerned. They suddenly thought of me as a friend, as one of them. What they didn't know is that I wasn't exactly the precision knife-thrower they thought I was and the fact that I didn't accidentally kill or maim him was just pure luck. I mean, I can stick a knife in a 30cm target from a few metres once in five attempts maybe, but this shot had surprised even me.

The theoretical part of the explosives course meant that you needed to know something about architecture and structural engineering, as you might be expected to park a vehicle loaded with explosives next to a building and it would be good to know where exactly to park, next to which supporting pillar it needed to be placed to cause the most possible damage. I was particularly good at this as my mother had taught structural engineering at a technical school, so I knew a fair bit about it.

The best part of training for Sanin and I was abseiling or rappelling off buildings. That is how I beat my fear of heights that was my biggest obstacle to fulfilling my life-long dream of becoming a pilot. Well, you could say there were some bigger obstacles but that was one of them. We enjoyed it so much that we put some improvised equipment together to abseil off buildings in the city centre during our free time.

Our abseiling instructor, Hussein, had been seriously wounded by then, thirty-nine times to be exact. He constantly showed off his naked plastic shoulder, while doing three hundred push-ups on one hand. Every night, when we didn't have night training, our instructors went to frontlines around town to kill people of other faiths, totally convinced that if they got killed themselves they would go straight to heaven to sexually abuse virgins.

Abaz was the most dangerous. He didn't talk much. He was verbal only in the morning before training when they talked about their activities from the night before. I didn't speak Arabic, but you could tell from their gesturing how and with what pleasure they had killed. You could sense every detail. Abaz's face would take on an expression of pride and sublimity, as if he had done a most noble thing. Then they would all laugh loudly when he recalled the last moments of his victim, mimicking their helpless facial expression just before dying. I was trying to comprehend how it was possible to find pleasure and happiness in killing. I was not far from working it out myself that day.

* * *

And then the sun went down.

"Your weed is great! What do you think about us creating a small diversion?", I suggested while stoned. "We'll take a few hand grenades, make a few tripwire mines and set them between our trenches and theirs?"

We peeled back the foil from some UN armoured plastic glass replacement in a window and pulled out the plastic wires from inside. We tied them together then tied the safety pins of hand grenades to one end and attached the other to a pointed stick. We used a second wire to tie leaves around the hand grenades for camouflage. These went in our rucksacks and after dark we set off towards their trenches. Relying solely on our sense of touch, we positioned the mines as we'd done in training so many times. Just then, however, one of the enemy soldiers thought of checking out the front line using infrared night vision optics and showered us with sharpened lead from what we called a *Sower of Death*.[4]

After some manoeuvring we managed to survive scratch free. That night the Orthodox Christians, provoked by our attempted attack, fired at us with everything they had. And they had a lot. It was one of the louder nights at that frontline. Our friend Digla lost his shin, hit by an explosive round from an anti-aircraft gun. Other than him, by a small wonder, there were no other casualties in our unit that night.

Early in the morning, the scout told us that the leaves on the grenades had dried and were peeling off, and that you could see them from miles away. And when we looked, it was exactly as he said. Our grenades were clearly sticking out from the even

---

4   7.62 mm machine gun firing a lethal twelve rounds per second.

colour of the grass. They were some hundred metres from the scout and not even ten from us. Last night it had seemed like we had crawled all the way to their trenches. When we were done laughing at ourselves and our rotten sense of space and distance, coupled with lousy knowledge of botany, we realised we had to take the grenades away before the Orthodox Christians started laughing at us as well. It was also quite possible that one of our guys could really get fucked up if we ever used this path to advance. Zhutyo, a nice friendly B&W dog that ran around there daily, could also get fucked. Well, we called him Zhutyo[5], they probably called him Srboljub[6] or something similar.

We immediately crawled out into the grass again and started de-mining. We had it done in no time. A couple of minutes. No one saw us. Why would they? As if there was anyone that crazy to look out into the meadow at that time of the day. If we hadn't planted the grenades, we wouldn't be looking at it ourselves either. No one would be stupid enough to attack during the day.

News of the two idiots springing into action on their own initiative spread throughout the brigade quite quickly. Soon the field telephone rang and the brigade commander asked to speak to me directly.

---

5   Zhutyo means yellow.
6   Srboljub – Archaic male name in the Balkans which translates as 'one who loves Serbs'.

Our brigade was led by a junkie, dealer, thief, pimp, gambler, racketeer and a murderer; today he is a very religious man but he is still a thief, gambler, racketeer and a murderer. A significant part of the BiH Army command was made up of similar types. The first 'combat' operations they ordered were to plunder anything and everything that could be stolen. Those small groups of criminals gradually grew into larger units. When Army of BiH was formed they joined the regular army, some having already grown to the brigade size. Each of these 'commanders' then took the part of the town that they had controlled before the war as well, called a 'zone of responsibility', where they could go unpunished whilst doing whatever came to their mind. And all sorts of things came to their minds. They weren't prosecuted for these activities after the war either.

"Idiot! Who told you to open up the front? Nobody does fuck all until I say so! Clear?"

"Yes, commander, but we were told they were going to attack, so I thought it makes no difference who starts. We thought of doing it again today. We have a feeling the Chetniks don't watch the line during the day. They just play rummy with cigarettes as chips, get high and drink, those Chetnik shits!"

"Ah, go fuck yourself!"

But in the tone of his voice, I thought I could hear a hint of approval.

* * *

And so at noon sharp, the two of us armed only with grenades and knives set off across the fire-swept zone. We had come up with the perfect plan. We'd go all the way into their trenches, because fuck it, they are not there. If they were, they would have killed us off this morning.

Sanin would take the right trench, and I'd take the left. Before we split, we gave each other a meaningful two second look of support, followed by the thumb up gesture meaning, "See you, bro. Good luck. We can do this; we are fucking killing machines. We do the job and we come back. Be brave, bro!" But right after separating, the subtext suddenly changed to, "What the fuck am I doing?"

Adrenaline hit me harder and harder. I was now wondering what if, unlike us, they were watching the line during the day as well?

As I crawled, I went through all the possible scenarios. I was thinking about the utterly dumb decision to take nothing but my rucksacks and a knife, not an automatic rifle, not even a fucking pistol, nothing to use to defend myself. I didn't even take a bottle of water. And that amazing knife. What the fuck do I need a knife for? I guess I'd use the knife to fight off the armada or did we go into Rambo mode during the training? Or maybe if caught alive, we'd stick the knife directly in our hearts, to end the suffering. Ah, yes, we took the knife in case we ran into one of their mines, we could then use that mine and knife trick from training. Smart idea to say the least!

I was wearing a camouflage uniform that was way too short and ripped up white All-star trainers which could be seen from a mile away. Snipers dream of these opportunities and such idiots as me. From any higher point one could easily see the trail of flattened grass I was leaving behind me like a snail. And there were higher points all around. The one comfort was that we hoped they wouldn't think idiots who'd try something like this at mid-day could exist.

The sun was at its zenith and I was soaked as I approached their trenches. I imagined how as I entered the trench, some bearded character with bloodshot eyes would grab my arm and scream like a savage showing his fangs as he rammed a bayonet through the top of my head, through the skull, turning it left and right few times, just for pleasure. With those beards, Chetniks always reminded me of those savages from A Southern Comfort. Same mindset implies same outfit I guess.

It was stupid to give up and even more so to panic thinking about the bearded guy. I knew that our guys were watching me from the observation post, and that they would see me all the way to the trench. And that if I gave up they would make fun of me until I died. In fact, it would be easier to die a painful death.

Each crawl became harder. I was feeling weak. Bad food, shortages of protein, minerals, and vitamins. Unbearable thirst, adrenaline hyperventilation, heat and fear were growing proportionally to each metre I covered and were making me stop and pause more frequently. The trench was very close now and I could already see the last stretch of grass before the clearing. I was nearly there, just a few metres to the goal, when I thought I heard the cocking of an automatic rifle. I ducked to the ground quickly and accidentally breathed in the dust through my dry throat and into each fucking alveolus. The urge to cough was intensifying and I had no saliva to swallow the dust. I just had to focus really hard on trying not to cough as if that happened I'd reveal my position, if I hadn't done so already. I took off my rucksack and turned onto my back, looking at the sky with my mouth wide open, trying to breathe slowly without irritating my throat, but my lungs were contracting by themselves and I looked like a cat trying to spit out a fur ball, just without the accompanying sound. This made me sweat and dehydrate even faster. Both my underwear and my socks were completely sweat-soaked now.

They say there are two things you can't hide; a lack of self-confidence and a cough. I had both at the same time. The first cough was the loudest. It came out of nowhere. It escaped without me even getting a chance to prepare for it. The rest I covered with my inner elbow, as we were taught during training, and coughed like crazy. I know it was bad timing but there was nothing I could do. I had a feeling that each and every cricket within a mile's radius stopped chirping to let me have a good hack and let everyone know exactly where I was. Now I was on my back, eyes shut, face tight, waiting for the bearded guy and ready for the worst. All he needs to do is reach out with his hand. Any time now. I am waiting. Now is the time. But nothing happened. Who knows how long I waited until I slowly opened one eye and tilted my head back slowly. I couldn't see anyone.

"Fuck this!" I repeated to myself, "Fuck this, fuck this, fuck this!"

I turned onto my belly and looked around frantically. To be honest, I didn't feel like going down there into their trench. I realized how much we had overestimated ourselves and how unprepared we were to be setting off on this adventure. But fuck it, enough with the whining, it was time to go in. I slowly looked over the edge and all I could see were ammo crates. Piles of ammo neatly stacked next to the wall, of a wide, machine-dug trench. I quickly turned feet first, jumped in and squatted between two rows of crates, peeking out fast to one side then the other. I was looking to see if they'd forgotten a

rifle; I could really use one. I could hear them clearly somewhere but couldn't tell how far away they
were. Were they in this trench around the corner or
somewhere further? I couldn't tell. Or was I hearing
things induced by fear? I was now so deep in shit
I would have loved to be anywhere else right now
just not here. In an absolute panic, I tied the loose
end of the fishing line to the root of a plant sticking
out of the ground and tried to pull out the pin out
of the grenade carefully and gently so it didn't come
out all the way. That would activate it in four or five
seconds, together with all these crates and me on
top, as I wasn't sure I would be able to get out of the
trench in time in the condition I was in. And even
if I did, I wouldn't get far. The pin needed to stay in
but also to be pulled out easily and the plant root
had already tightened the fishing line at the other
end. I had another problem now, as if I didn't have
enough problems already. I couldn't let the grenade
out of my hand but instead had to use my other hand
to release the fishing line from the root and wrap it
again, bearing in mind the length and tension of the
line. Fuck, this was now taking way too long. I tried
to push the pointed stick with a grenade on into the
ground next to the crate but the ground was so dry
and hard that every time I pushed it only went about
a millimetre deep. I eventually wedged it somehow
horizontally between the wooden crates. There was
no way I'd manage to place the second grenade but

never mind. This one was in the right place. When the next person came down to the trench we should hear 'Kaboom!' I checked it all once more. Then I stood on one of the crates and just about managed to climb out of the trench with my hands. Without looking back, I started running, actually wobbling zig-zags towards our trenches. Fuck the crawling. Run for your life!

Our scout saw it all. He confirmed and spread the news. We were heroes that day. I went to the field hospital to change the wet shirt. Alma, my commander's girlfriend, the one he left his wife and kids for, was ogling me.

"You're crazy!" She smiled at me mischievously, overtly flirtatious. So I fucked her.

Everyone congratulated us. Me and Sanin, that is. Not me and her.

* * *

"They will recommend us to be decorated with the Golden Lily[7]. That's what they are saying," Sanin said.

"Wow! We really did it!"

---

7   The Order of the Golden Lily was the highest decoration of the Army of BiH. It was a gold pin that many secretaries of the ruling party received, as well as their relatives and friends, without ever having much to talk about in terms of the combat experience. The fighters who received it because they deserved it often sold it as second-hand gold to jewellers after the war to buy food.

* * *

I'm not sure why I am always so fascinated by the sunset. Early in the evening, even though I was exhausted, I was on my shift in the same trench watching the perfection again, listening to Sanin's war stories about today's action without really focusing. I was thinking how someone, somewhere, not far perhaps a hundred or so kilometres from here, was watching the same sunset, with the same sun but from the deck of a cruise ship. He was getting a martini with ice, sipping and thinking, "Three more instalments and the Porsche will be paid off. Damn those loans, they are a real headache". Well... I could also have been on that cruise ship but...

Booooom! There was an unusual explosion that shook the ground and thick black smoke started coming up over their trench. Almost instantaneously, shooting towards us started from all sides. First infantry, then with great noise, pieces of wood, earth, metal and everything we detonated began falling down on us from above. A few seconds later, their artillery started with its favorite and only tactic: flatten anything and everything from a safe distance. Retaliation was brutal; thousands of 120mm mortars, hundreds of tank and howitzer projectiles came our way changing geography again.

My two-hour shift in the trench was over and my four hours of break time were coming up. I needed to use that time to sleep. Comrades came crawling and running, to take our place. They told me that they have no information on casualties so far, except few lightly wounded on our side, but that they have heard over the radio that Zhutyo the dog had set off the mine I placed.

"Not Zhutyo, for fuck sake, why? Why fucking Zhutyo?"

I ran across to the ruined house that we slept in and went to bed in the dark cellar room. Everything was fucked up. My comrades were in the other room, playing rummy with cigarettes as chips as always, drinking homemade Raki 'liberated' from one of the nearby Orthodox Christian's houses and using a car light connected to a car battery to see. They were talking about our action today. They hadn't noticed me enter and carried on as before.

"He is crazy, I thought that from day one. Fucking special forces! Now we'll all get killed because of their fucking about!"

"Fedja is a good guy but I always have him in my sights", said my platoon commander.

And so I started feeling rather depressed. The feeling of victory and a bit of heroic pleasure from earlier all vanished. My platoon commander, for whom I would have given my life without even thinking a minute ago, has me in his sights! Perhaps because of my non-Muslim name? Well, fuck you all, Muslims, Orthodox and Catholics! I killed Zhutyo today, who sat by my feet in the trench so many times during shelling, shivering with fear, together with me. He didn't quite get it was war, he didn't understand that up there outside his micro world, there was hatred to the point of extinction. He could recognise the vibration of the exact mortar that was aimed at our position, then he'd whine and run in circles until we all hid. Zhutyo saved hundreds of lives like that. He didn't know that we were divided in Muslims, Orthodox and Catholics, ready to kill for myths and infertile land that he ran across freely, crossing from ours to theirs and back. He loved us all. For him we were all the same, he didn't ask our names. I killed him today. Sorry Zhutyo. Sorry my only brother. Fuck this war.

Last night I could have easily killed a human being and in doing so, helped mine and his lot in piss-marking this looted territory, well-camouflaged with religion and patriotism. They had long ago made me into a hypnotised monkey, blinded with hate, ready to kill for the rich, for those who sent their kids to expensive schools? But that was not me anymore. You were not the first I shot at but bro, you'll be the last. I am not shooting at anyone, for anyone or anything anymore. Bring your children instead. Bring your children to fight for your family business and your gods, and they can proudly roll in the mud and blood for a while. Excuse me but I really have some better things to do.

Alma said I was crazy. Everyone did, actually. Everyone still thinks I'm crazy. Well, I am crazy. I liked the idea. I am crazy or actually, I will be crazy. Decision made then, this was my last day in the army!

The shelling went on with the same intensity until 11pm. As usual, it stopped suddenly on order. Unplanned, an hour later reinforcements arrived to relieve us. I have a feeling they were sent just to move the two of us out of there.

* * *

Street fighting went on in the city that night. Caco, the commander of one of the brigades and a war criminal famous for his brutal killings of non-Muslim civilians in Sarajevo, killed nine police officers that day. Almost all Muslims. Almost all were of my age. Just kids. He dug their eyes out, mutilated the bodies and threw them off the first floor of his headquarters. Police, with couple of army special units, attacked his brigade and caught him. The father of one of the murdered police officers took him out. Even after all these serious crimes, he was buried as a hero with the highest Islamic honours.

* * *

My mother was awake waiting for me and was happy to see me again.

"Son!", she kissed me on both cheeks, "You're alive! How was the frontline?"

"It was OK, no big deal. Look, I'm going to go to the hospital tomorrow, to the psychiatric unit, and if it works, come and see me. And if the military police look for me, tell them where I am. If it doesn't work, I'll be home for lunch."

"Good luck my son, love you".

* * *

"Good afternoon, I am crazy. I can hear voices. They tell me I need to kill all my comrades. I don't know what to do!"

They tied me to a bed and injected me with 150ml of Largactil in the buttocks. And that was the start of a brand new war altogether.

* * *

Largactil is a very serious drug. When on it, you can't sleep, eat, lie down or think. I was given it three times a day. On top of that, they injected me with Haloperidol Decanoate for twenty-one days and as a result, I was soon no different to anyone else in there.

My mother came to visit me three days later. She couldn't come sooner because the city was under heavy artillery fire. I mean even heavier than usual. She sat by my bed and looked at me with sadness.

"Mother, get me out of here, please! I want to go to war! I can't spend another hour here!"

"Hang on son," she said.

Jozo was a nice, middle-aged, tall, skinny paranoid schizophrenic who had massacred his parents with a knife twenty years earlier because "they tried to kill me" by "tampering with the brakes on my bicycle." He hadn't been out of the ward P1 since then. He came up to us and said, "Fedja had a great night's sleep last night. I was stealing cigarettes from his locker all night long and he didn't notice anything!"

"It doesn't seem to be so bad here," my mother said, laughing. I didn't have the strength to reply to that.

You could hear all sorts of inarticulate screams from somewhere in the distance but there was one that stood out, as nonstop for three days it kept repeating: "Majydah, mom, dad! Majydah, mom, dad! Majydah, mom, dad..."

* * *

The intensive care unit of the psychiatric ward was a mixed-gender ward for the hardest cases. It was accessed through the P1 ward, a men's ward with patients classified as non-aggressive so not usually tied down. There were twenty patients in each of the three large rooms in P1, situated in the old and decrepit part of the building. Further down the long corridor was the intensive care ward and that part of the building was quite modern. There was a large glass room on the left side with a wall dividing it into two parts with two beds in each. It was separated from the corridor by thick armoured glass; the shop window. The hardest cases were there. At the end of the corridor was a wide room, split into three sections with two beds in each. I was in the middle section. I could see the whole corridor from there; the ten beds for the ten craziest patients in the whole country. It all stank terribly of human waste as patients that were tied down to the bed often defecated right there. In the morning, they'd line up next to the radiator to dry their pyjamas, while they were still full of shit. There was an armoured window above my head through which, when I wasn't tied down, I could see Poljine, one of the worst of the enemy strongholds, some three or four kilometres away.

Five or six days later, the military police came to see me together with the brigade doctor. They looked at me, realised I wasn't faking it and left.

The first few months were the hardest. The therapy was killing me.

One day an armour-piercing shell flew into the ward section on my right. Fragments of concrete killed patient Drago and his madman roommate. I didn't feel anything in particular regarding the event. I was glad to be alive myself. For the first time, there was silence in the madhouse. There wasn't even "Majydah, mom, dad!", for a good five minutes. A bunch of loonies from P1 came to my section to see what was happening but nurse Srechko sent them off. Jesus Christ was talking rubbish about the apocalypse, as usual. He was doing it ever so loudly this time with great gestures, encouraged that his claims were true, literally by concrete evidence. So Srechko punched him on the forehead, after which he fell asleep and started snoring instantaneously. It was very funny, made my day. I have to admit Jesus was quite convincing. Maybe he was the real Jesus but no one took him seriously, which was probably for the best for him. When you are delusional about being Jesus Christ you end up in here with me. When you hallucinate about his mother you become rich and famous.

The two unlucky ones were taken to the morgue some hundred metres from the nuthouse. Builders were fixing the wall the whole day with nurses and cleaners cleaning the dust. Then they placed two new mattresses on beds and tied two new patients to them, so normal life went on.

* * *

One morning a new guy appeared in the bed next to mine, twenty years old or so. He wasn't tied down but was so heavily sedated that he appeared dead. His wrists were bandaged so I assumed he had attempted suicide. He had probably suffered significant blood loss. Srechko came to see him from time to time and when the new guy showed some sign of life, Srechko would inject more of something into his IV, and the guy would drift into a coma again.

The creaking of a hospital bed woke me that night. Jozo was raping the new patient. I was tied and could do nothing but call Srechko, the nurses or doctors. I screamed as loudly as I could. Then there was a sound of the key turning in the heavy metal door. Jozo stopped the raping, jumped away from the bed, pulled up his pyjama bottoms and went back off towards the P1 ward. Srechko ran in with a full syringe. He ran straight past Jozo, threw himself on top of me and injected me in the buttocks. I woke up in the section behind the armoured glass. I didn't mention rape to anyone. They'd call me crazy.

Kemo, the guy who had been saying "Majydah, Mom, Dad", constantly for a month, was my new room mate.

* * *

The military police and the brigade doctor visited me regularly. Although I was permitted to spend a night at home during the weekend with a signature from one of my parents, I didn't do it so as to avoid missing them if they came to see me.

When he saw me in the room behind the armoured glass, the brigade doctor said to me that in his opinion, I was no longer capable of army duty and that he would recommend to the higher military evaluation board that I should be discharged. But he didn't know my diagnosis so he asked my doctor. She said that I was still under observation and that I would soon be given a diagnosis. I needed a good one, the one that gets you an army discharge.

* * *

Twice a week we had medical students visit our ward. They spent most of their time in front of our shop window. They'd look at us, point at things, whisper among themselves and write things down. Kemo was saying his usual thing and sometimes I'd throw a pack of cigarettes at them or scratch at the glass with a cretin face on just to make things more interesting for them. Then they would talk among themselves some more, write more things down and compare notes thus determining my diagnosis.

One night, I was woken up by the doctor. She untied me and asked me to come to her office at the end of the P1 corridor.

"The guys from your brigade are asking me for a diagnosis and I don't know what to tell them."

"Doctor, I'm not crazy. I am here to get away from the frontline. I am sane."

"Sure you are. All of you here are sane and normal. Tell me about yourself, your childhood. How did you get here?"

"My childhood? Well, if I had one at all... My father Mustafa and my mother Nadja, renowned architects by the way and yes, my sister Eni is an architect too, them and the extended family could not find common ground. I can't remember too many nice things from my childhood. There were nice things, I know that, but rarely. Mostly, throughout my childhood I felt a mixture of sorrow, anxiety, injustice, helplessness, loneliness and fear. I was constantly trying to figure out why people do what they do to each other and in doing so, to those who are not to blame for the predicament or for anything else. Why do they create a life that they shit on later? What's the trick there?

People felt strange to me since I was born. The first time that I ran away from home was when I was five. Mind you, I was quickly caught then, just two streets down from mine. It was lucky I had a good gang of friends outside the house. We already had a band in the second year of primary school; Hamo, Muamer, Haris, Migula and Kole. That's when I started smoking and then a few years later, drinking as well. When I was with the gang, I didn't think of home as that was inevitably where shit awaited. My thoughts went there only as I was putting in the key to unlock the doors. As I did so, I hoped maybe things behind them wouldn't be that bad. Hope is the last to die.

I trained my brain not to think of the shit at home and then life could be beautiful. Parents of my friends were not too pleased that they were hanging out with me. They used to tell them, "Don't be like Fedja. Study and get a degree". For them I was someone who was certain to become a nobody. I thought that quite often too but not in a pejorative way and it didn't upset me much either. The prognosis for me was bleak as I did actually want to become a nobody. Without society's shackles, norms and morals. That was my definition of freedom; to be a 'nobody', not a moulded form of successful homo sapiens. I was streaming towards full submission to uncertainty without an aim. I already knew then that it wouldn't be easy and that I would always chose the harder path. Very early on I decided to try everything there was to try. They say that every decision in life is made 1 to 5 seconds before a person sees it as *their own idea, meaning that you can't really call it free will nor freedom of choice. So I decided nothing, it did it all before even asking for my opinion. The brain that is. And it seemed to be interested in real life only. It liked knowledge but never purely because it was forced to know something. I never could stand authority. I don't hate it; I simply have no respect for it. This strong fixation based on a well-founded childhood aversion is why I am here. Because of freedom. I wanted to fly. I've always dreamed of being a pilot or a parachutist and it wasn't just a childhood dream, it is an obsession. As a child, I went on a trip with my mum. My first flight ever. The memory is still so vivid, as if it was this morning. I became a pilot that day in my mind. Ever since then I had been looking up at the sky, knowing my desire was unattainable, so I found a replacement instead. I started drinking and doing drugs because they said it felt like flying.*

I grew up in a tough neighbourhood and first saw a murder while I was in the fifth grade, during break time. I remember it was three stabs to the heart. Later with the gang, I stole cars and broke into newsagents just for the sake of adrenaline. We used to steal lollipops and chewing gum, then later cigarettes. I tried playing pool and realized by chance that I had a great talent at it so I left high school to play professionally. From the age of thirteen up to seventeen I spent most of my time in smoky pool bars, playing with different bands at the same time. I also sometimes worked as a waiter when I needed money. At the beginning of 1991 I went to Kotor in Montenegro and that's where I met Sanja. She had just graduated from the Faculty of Maritime Studies and spoke eight languages. She had sailed the world four times, ran a private nursery and a restaurant. She was three times state champion in board-sailing and drove a Honda CBR 1000f. I fell in love with her and the Honda. She was eight years older than me, Sanja that is not the Honda. True love. The real thing. There was love before her, the boyish type, but this was different; the kind of love that prevents you doing anything but loving. It was a totally destabilising love that meant looking at the stars at night and kicking the rustling leaves in the park.

I got a job as a waiter in a pool bar. I practiced non-stop, won tournaments and played for money. That's how I earned the money to stay with her. I once made so much money playing pool against some boxers from Loznica that I could buy a new Volkswagen Golf. Except that because they were not very sportsmanlike about their loss, I had to give it all back. It was the last time I played for money I think. The war had begun in Slovenia already and shit was kicking off in Croatia too.

A Ukrainian band played at the club every night. They had five singers who were actually prostitutes. Since I knew quite a lot of people around town they asked me to be their pimp and I agreed. The only customer I ever found them was my friend Mujo. I brought him to Nataša and he later married her. After a month of bad business, the remaining four Ukrainians fucked me off and found a new pimp.

By then, they were were mobilising men fit capable of military service in Montenegro and sending them to the battlefields of Croatia.[8] But that all seemed so far away. Besides, I was in love and not paying much attention to the war although Dubrovnik was only some sixty kilometres away as the crow flies.

Then there was a shooting at the club and the police caught me with someone else's gun which I had used to shoot at some idiot from Vršac in Serbia. I didn't kill him as the gun was a Magnum 357 revolver with three good bullets and three that were already fired. All you heard when I pulled the trigger was, "click, click!". I thought that the gun was faulty but when they gave me a slip for temporary confiscation of property, I realised how lucky I was by accidentally trying to fire the spent rounds, as well as how lucky the idiot from Vršac was. Especially him really!

---

8   While the majority of population in socialist republics of Slovenia, Croatia, Bosnia and Herzegovina and Macedonia voted for sovereignty at referendums, ethnic Serbs in those republics voted to remain part of Yugoslavia. Serbia and Montenegro, acting jointly at the time and misusing JNA, incited local Serbs in those republics to turn against other ethnic groups in order to forcefully prevent their secessions. Thanks to the low number of ethnic Serbs, separation of North Macedonia went peacefully. Later on Montenegro gained its sovereignty.

But, regardless, they could have convicted me of attempted murder with a maximum penalty of six years imprisonment. I was detained with a couple of Romanian thieves. They were both constantly flipping a razor blade in their mouths, half a razor each, actually. I was dreading that I would wake up one morning with my throat slit but the razors had a different purpose; the opening of handcuffs. They taught me the skill. When I ran away from my trial, the new skill proved particularly useful.

It was a hot day when four policemen took me through the crowd on the main square to the court-room. Three of the policemen went into the court-room and the fourth was at the door, waiting for the judge to call for me. He stood at the door, looking at the judge and waiting. But I didn't wait. I saw an opportunity and took off, got on a bus and came to Sarajevo. I didn't dare go to Sanja to say goodbye as I assumed they'd be looking for me there.

In Sarajevo, one of three the ruling parties, the SDA[9], was already re-selling weapons to the people, weapons that they'd bought from our future enemy[10]. It was their first dirty job.

JNA jet planes were breaking the sound barrier above the city, scaring people and giving us an

---

9   Muslim Nationalist Party
10 all the infantry weapons in Army of BiH were manufactured at the Crvena Zastava, armaments factory in Kragujevac, Serbia

introduction to what was to come. They were digging trenches around the city and bringing artillery in for months, whilst telling the press it was just a military exercise. I was one of those who believed it too. We didn't believe in a war. Us, the people from the cities. We didn't make any distinctions based on ethnicity or religion. We couldn't even tell the names apart. But in smaller places in the countryside these things had always been well known. That was where the hatred came from. It resulted from frustration, bad education, low living standards and a lack of activities, I guess. And religion. For them the idea of a war caused euphoria, as if it were the greatest thing ever to happen to them.

Then a member of a Serbian wedding party got killed.

The murder was ordered to provoke the war I guess. The killer was one of the main characters from the narco-cartels and was not arrested but instead became a brigade commander. He was not held responsible for the murder after the war either. At least not before the law. He was eventually sprayed with bullets and killed in front of his apartment. And those perpetrators were never found.

Then came the first barricades. The first shots were fired. The first heads covered in balaclavas. It became clearer to me that something was being prepared, something very real, but at that point I could not even imagine the extent of what was to come. I bought a Scorpio, an automatic gun similar to an Uzi but made in Serbia, which was later confiscated of course, for the needs of the army.

Sanja was saying we should go abroad somewhere and that I could get a job on a cruise ship or a tanker using her connections. I wasn't too keen since I wasn't sure if there was an international arrest warrant with my name on it. I couldn't just go to the police and ask: "Excuse me, could you check if I'm wanted by Interpol?"

Until things calmed down, I got a job at an art gallery selling paintings. I knew the history of art by heart since my family had suffocated me with it since the day I was born.

Then I got a subpoena stating my trial would commence on 6 April 1992 in Sarajevo. The demonstrations in front of parliament started that day. Some snipers shot at the people protesting and the war started. How lucky was I!

A few thousand of us went into the parliament building and stayed there for few couple of days. I still spoke to Sanja on the phone until 2 May 1992, when the Orthodox fired an incendiary mortar at the main post office, cutting off all phone traffic for a long time. That was one of the worst days of the war. Sometime around noon, the street fighting started.

Earlier that day, I had asked my friend Nadir to buy me a pack of Marlboros. Some ten days later I found out that he was hit by shrapnel cutting the artery in his thigh, whilst in front of the newsagent. He bled out on the way to the hospital. He was one of the first casualties of the war.

The JNA was withdrawing from the city and moving up into the surrounding hills. As they pulled out, the shelling started. It sounded like an ongoing detonation only changing in intensity with each second and lasting until just before dawn.

I hid in the cellar of the nearby hotel Europe that survived ten direct artillery hits that night. I climbed up one of the floors and crawled through the corridors over pieces of bricks and glass, through smoke and dust. A few rooms were on fire. In one of the rooms I found a phone on the floor and I dialed Sanja's number.

"Hello?", she said.

"Sanja, it's me..." At that moment, the phones in the city stopped working and that was the last I heard of her: "Hello?".

In the morning, when the shelling stopped, I left the hotel and set off home. The city was one big ruin. Buildings were on fire. There was a horrid smell of burning and gunpowder. That's how war smells.

There were bricks and shards of glass everywhere. Wounded, bloodied people were coming out of the cellars crying and moaning, going somewhere to get help, I guess. It was both terrifying and incredibly sad.

Then I fought for a secular, modern state because that was the story back then. I had no idea this would become an Islamic state (and by that I don't mean ISIS but an ethnically clean Muslim territory), although it seems now that that was the hidden plan from the start. Or maybe not. It seems hardly anyone here had a plan other than looting.

I enlisted in the police along with my brother-in-law Radenko, as that was the only regular armed force at the time.

One day I convinced my comrade Huso to stay after his shift to play another round of chess. After the round, Huso left the building and was killed by a grenade.

We were a team; we went into actions together. Hmm, actions?! They would put us in an armoured yellow postal van; you could see it from miles away. We didn't know where we were going nor where the enemy was. Once in broad daylight, they took us to Poljine (the hill you could see from the nuthouse).

I got issued a double-barreled hunting shotgun which I found out ten days later did not work at all when I tried to return fire at a truck that they were shooting at me from.

Who knows how many other weapons were malfunctioning? We mostly got issued the M48 rifle from just after the Second World War and some PAP semi-automatic rifles and those certainly weren't weapons that someone would send you to make an attack with. We only had three automatics between us, the AK47s, because what would we need them for, since we were not there to fight but just to be killed. And if we were to get killed it would be a good opportunity to get rid of the old and malfunctioning weapons.

Machine-gun and sniper fire was tearing us apart. Our fucking fluorescent van was hit hundreds of times. The sound of a bullet hitting that closed up tin echoed hard and caused quite a panic in the dark. The closer we were to the battlefield, the more bullets penetrated the 5mm thin steel plate, leaving as a result a straight and narrow, shining ray of sunlight through the disturbed dust. Then, with a loud metal bang, they bounced off the opposite plate and around the interior of the van. We laid on the floor, one on top of the other, screaming helplessly.

They threw us out near some old ruined house. I was the first to run inside; Radenko followed and then the others. Then the heavy artillery joined in. From the house we watched how brave fighters of our sold-out army were dying. Dozens of them. It was a scene like the Normandy landings. Fuck this! I knew we would all be killed if only a single shell hit the house, so I ran through the window. Radenko followed and then all the others. Screaming. A shell did indeed hit the house and erased it off the face of the earth just a few seconds after the last soldier left. We hid in the maternity hospital that was quite wrecked already. I thought how I was born there and how, ironically, I would end my life there too. My brother-in-law and I were telling stupid jokes and killing ourselves with laughter. That was a reaction to panic and fear. A mortar shell exploded at the end of the corridor we were in, just thirty metres from us, and blew two men from another unit to pieces. We were merely covered in dust, bruised and disoriented due to the explosion of the 155mm projectile. We couldn't hear anything other than loud whistling for a long time. That kind of detonation makes you feel as if you were hit by a car. We were touching ourselves in disbelief, searching for shrapnel holes, but all we kept finding were pieces of the two dead men. Then the artillery went silent. We couldn't hear it as our hearing was damaged but we felt the ground stop shaking.

Chetniks were surrounding the hospital and the only way to save ourselves was to try to run through a minefield. Our chances of survival were close to zero but still better than if we stayed there.

We ran screaming. Shells were ploughing into the soft earth and their explosions threw us all over the minefield. The waistband on my tracksuit broke *due to the weight of the ammunition in my pockets and I had to hold it up with one hand while running for my life. If they were watching me through sniper sights at that moment, they probably didn't shoot me because they were laughing so hard.*

We got to the outskirts of the city and hid in a building. No one in my unit was even scratched. Actually, we were quite scratched and bleeding, but in one piece. Most others didn't do as well that day.

Later the story was told how the Grand Mufti, the Islamic leader, had a dream in which we would win a great victory if we attacked Poljine and that is why the assault was ordered. This information is not verified but is quite probably true.

Grand Mufti was some sort of wizard who would predict the outcomes of battles or the war itself. He had a great influence in this part of the country. The Islamic community is the right hand of the ruling body as it secures votes during elections. This goes for all three of the dominant religions in the divided territories. The steering board of the Islamic community has politicians from the ruling party on it: one of them was charged (then acquitted) of stealing 390 million marks (some $200 million) from the state budget. Such staged court processes actually serve as amnesty, or legalisation of theft since the accused can't be tried twice for the same crime. Once acquitted, the perpetrator is a free man and millions, taken from the taxpayers, become his legally acquired capital. All politicians of any importance in the country have been through this procedure of money laundering via court acquittals. Judges who acquit them also get their cut.

I remember clearly the confused looks on the faces of our commanders when we returned to base. Shock and disbelief, such an unpleasant surprise – followed by badly faked happiness that we had returned alive. Stuttering, avoiding visual contact, swallowing of saliva, sweating, disproportional gesticulation, forced laughter and all the other textbook signs of a bad liar caught in his attempted deceit. These kind of things don't really boost the morale. I saw the question in their eyes; 'What the fuck are you doing here? How do we explain this to our superiors now?'

Commanders don't usually take part in combat. They get promotions, medals, apartments and business spaces. It seemed they didn't partake in war at all. This was probably the biggest reason for the very low morale in our army and why the defensive lines around the city never moved an inch forward. 'We've been sold out', was the most often used phrase by soldiers after every battle I took part in. And the list of battles was quite long, as they sent us everywhere and always without a chance of succeeding. Our actions always had the same ending: running away for the lucky ones and a bunch of unlucky corpses.

I dated the daughter of the Special Brigade commander for few months and I was there when from his home he directed an action resulting in forty-eight dead. Among them, two of my friends and a few acquaintances.

Later on, the story was told (and this is not confirmed but is quite possible) that all those people were shot in the back by members of Ševe – mercenary units composed of the biggest scum in the region.

We were once sent to battle in the Otes settlement in Sarajevo suburbia. We were attacked by members of the 63rd Parachute Brigade or Turtle-Men as we called them, the best trained and equipped of the elite JNA special forces. They were wearing head-to-toe body armour and carrying heavy machine-guns. M84[11] tanks were their escort and we could do nothing to them.

---

11 The M84 tank with active armour automatically fired back towards the location it was fired at from, while destroying RPG mortars and rockets from hand-held launchers on the go with machine-gun fire. The only way to disable it was to fire three projectiles at it from three different sides at the same time.

The number of civilians and soldiers killed in this attack was never officially disclosed. We managed to escape to the fallback position. The old slaughterhouse.

One day, as we were sitting in the slaughterhouse cellar, I offered my seat to an elderly soldier who had just returned from guard duty. As soon as he sat down, a splinter of shrapnel the size of grain of rice went through a small improvised ventilation shaft in the wall, between his eyes and into his skull. He died instantly. Before going into battle, he'd always show bunch of hospital papers to our commander to prove he was unfit for duty but it never worked. The commander always said, "If he can move his index finger," gesturing the motion of pulling a trigger, "He is good to go."

The whole building above us was on fire constantly. Barrels filled with lard were burning.

We spent fifteen days there and no one even bothered to send a relief. They told us to stay there because we knew the terrain well, but the real truth was that the relief unit was mainly political party people.

Eventually, I got pissed off and deserted. For a month I was nowhere. I hid from the military police at my friend's cellar or sat in the bar that the military police frequented. I was safe there. I counted on them thinking nobody without valid paperwork would ever dare go to that bar, so they never checked my papers. Still, I had to register somewhere so I enlisted in the brigade that all my childhood friends were in. I never saw them at the frontline as we were on opposite shifts. That brigade then sent me onto a specialist unit course held by the Mujaheddin and I slowly started to feel like an atheist in a Muslim army.

After the training, I performed a crazy action and everyone thought I was insane. I almost got the Golden Lily but... I killed a dog and they don't give out Lilies for animal pound duties, just for killing people. And so that gave me the idea to get out of the army using insanity as an excuse, as this war contradicted my religious beliefs. I am not crazy. I just wanted to get out of there and be with Sanja – doesn't matter if she's officially my enemy now. I love her.

"I can see you are OK," she said. "I'll diagnose you tomorrow. And, good luck, no one ever got away on an insanity plea."

"Thank you, and please stop this medication, it's unbearable!"

After the medication stopped life got much better. Friends came to visit every day. They had come before but I didn't register that while on the meds. I got on the good side of the nurses, and they didn't tie me down anymore. I sometimes even went with them to help tie other patients down. I used to change the catheter of an old lady with catatonic schizophrenia and she seemed to quite like me because of that. I thought so because she used to come to my bed each night, naked. I'd just push her off the bed onto the floor and continue sleeping. She had very long, yellow nails both on her hands and feet.

I gave the paperwork to the brigade doctor and all I could do then was wait. Diagnosis: emotionally immature, psychopathic, PTSD, psychoneurosis and a few others I can't remember any more. On their own they were not sufficient to get me out of the army but all together they could just do the trick.

* * *

Months passed. People changed or were killed. The worst was a suicide of a girl who slit her throat with a piece of a broken mirror. That was in a section next to mine in the same room. She bled out on the floor before anyone could do anything. The whole room was full of blood. I helped clean up. The speed of it all was unbelievable: suicide, cleaning and return to the usual routine. In fifteen minutes, no one was even thinking about it. Life lost all meaning. Alive or dead, totally irrelevant.

* * *

In the morning, Sejo filled her place. I immediately knew he was faking it like me. It was one of the nicest times in the nuthouse. I finally had someone to talk normally to. My granny slept across from Sejo. The first thing Sejo would see after he woke up was the naked granny. As soon as he opened his eyes, he would start swearing and moaning. He would then sit on my bed to light up just so he wouldn't have to look at her. I would then take the granny by the arm and bring her back to my bed, saying, "Do you like my new girlfriend?". He'd always go crazy over that but luckily for him, Granny died soon after. That same day I cut her nails off.

* * *

My volunteer work at the psychiatric clinic resulted in me taking an interest in that branch of medicine. By the end of my stay there, I could determine the diagnosis for a patient with great accuracy. And in my head of course, come up with the best treatment for them. My first patient was Kemo.

I had the keys to magnetic restraints to untie the patients when they wanted to use the toilet, so nurses wouldn't have to come and do that. I didn't tie down Kemo. He started guards' duties next to my bed. He'd wake me up at night with:

"General, general! Someone is coming, what should I do?"

"Ask for the code word and let him pass."

He'd then ask for an imaginary code word from a nurse, a doctor or some other patient from P1. I liked that. After few days of intense conversations with him, Kemo recovered fully. The man just needed to have a good chat, nothing more than that. He told me later that Madžida was his ex-wife whom he caught with a lover and then he lost it. Kemo, the patient with the most serious condition in intensive care, was released and I stayed for God knows how much longer.

I started thinking about what I could do one day if I got out of all of this alive. I could become a psychiatrist!

* * *

My friend Narda came to visit. She was studying drama.

"You should enroll in Drama Academy. You've fooled so many psychiatrists, you must be talented. I'll bring you two monologues, the audition is on Sunday so you have few days to prepare."

I had never thought about being an actor but the idea seemed cool. Acting or psychiatry, what's the difference?

I spent the whole of Saturday preparing for the audition. I was loudly reciting monologues while pacing up and down the corridor and no one thought I was being at all strange. On Sunday, my mother got me out by signing for me. I auditioned and passed!

* * *

And that's how I am in this business. So, how come I am at this hotel? Hmmm, here goes...

* * *

They put a new patient in Kemo's bed. The man was the spitting image of Woody Harrelson. Never have I seen such resemblance. He was brought in by four men, kicking and screaming. They barely managed to tie him to the bed.

Magnetic restraints are unbreakable. We were tied with them around our wrists and ankles with a wide one across the stomach. There was no moving. During one schizophrenic episode, even tied like that, Woody managed to turn the bed upside down before they were able to tie the restraint across his belly. He was just hanging upside down and screaming. I was in great fear. Since Kemo had left, the nights were quiet. Just sometimes you'd hear my new neighbour whisper very softly to himself, "Nurse, I'll drink your blood". I believed every word of it. One morning during a doctor's visit, I said that I was afraid of being next to Woody, hoping they'd move him. Instead they moved me to P1, in a room with nineteen loonies.

It was the kind of nuthouse you see in the movies. It stank even worse than I thought was possible. A few months later, the brigade doctor came and gave me my army passbook. On one of the pages it said, "Unfit for military service". I cannot describe the sheer joy I felt. FREEDOM! At that moment, however strange it sounds, I was the freest man on the planet. I was the first person to get out of the army by pleading insanity. I had a paper in my pocket that everybody envied but for patriotic reasons, they could never admit to it.

* * *

As I hadn't finished high school, I found a connection to get me a diploma for 500 Deutsche Marks which I submitted to the Academy of Performing Arts and started studying. The wonderful world of corruption. It was a different life altogether. I was in a class with six women. We performed, fucked about, went out and drank. The bars were always full, even though there was no power or water. A cassette player hooked up to a car battery, soft music, bad rice beer, candles and romance.

I could not believe there was something as good as acting was. Something to remove you so much from reality. It was occupational therapy for me who had wanted to be anything else but myself for most of my life. It was so much fun. People speaking like Master Yoda. For me, the war was over!

The ruling party decided to only distribute a small part of the humanitarian aid they received. They were to sell us the rest, highly priced on the black market. That was their second big job. I know that because when I was not on the frontline, I was guarding the largest warehouse of humanitarian aid. Trucks used to come early in the morning to take the supplies that would actually be distributed and at night it was much busier because of the vans from the market coming to get stuff. I stopped the air traffic twice by shooting towards the airport when planes with aid were landing. The Serbs did that to wear us out with hunger. I did it to stop the theft. If I need to answer to anybody because of that, I'm here and ready!

The small part we used to get was mainly flour, which we exchanged for alcohol. Then we got rice which we made into raki, pie, paté, Nutella, beer or even coffee. We also got tins of Mackerel, whose contents even the starving dogs wouldn't eat. Sometimes we got US Army ration portions, that you could also get in exchange for 300ml of blood at the Institute for Blood Transfusion or buy at the market. Everyone grew weed on their balconies and windows and either smoked it or exchanged it for goods. Parties were crazy. Crazier ever before or after. All of us were high on adrenaline 24/7. We lived as every day was our last because maybe it was and we were lewd to the max.

We went to our classes through a rain of bullets and shellfire.

* * *

Once on my way to the Academy, an old lady nearly fell on my head as she decided to take her own life right at that moment. She hit the sidewalk just a couple of metres in front of me, face down. I saw from the corner of my eye that something was falling from above and stopped for a second. The sound was terrifying, I can still hear it clearly. The ground shook. My classmates thought it was a mortar that hadn't exploded. The old lady's husband came out and knelt in the puddle of blood that was quickly spreading from her nose and mouth and I covered her with a blanket that some granny handed over.

* * *

People were dying all around. I can't even remember how many times I've picked up body parts off the street. It was a routine. Corpses and body parts went to the same pile. The wounded were put in a car. Later on staff came from the morgue to pick up the dead and the body parts. Sometimes there were leftovers for the stray dogs, mostly full-breed dogs abandoned due to food shortages and since gone wild. I once saw a dog running down the street with a human fist in his mouth after a massacre, joyfully wagging his tail. In all that horror, that was a scene that actually brought a smile to my face. I don't expect anyone's understanding on this and I am not asking for it either. That is just how it was. Each and every day. It was rough the first few times but one gets used to everything except children being killed. I never got used to that.

Once I caught myself trying to dig out dried blood from under my fingernails, with my teeth. It was the blood of an elderly lady, whose intestines I was trying to put back into her stomach fifteen minutes earlier. And failed. People have a lot of intestines that are unexpectedly heavy and slippery. The dominating colour on a mutilated and ripped body is not red as I used to think, but yellowish, off-white and a lighter shade of red. Before she lost consciousness, she tried to help me with the hand she still had holding her insides. She looked at me pleading, as if I could save her life. Then she closed her eyes half-way. I am no expert in medicine but I do know when someone is dead. I placed the intestines that kept falling out next to her in the trunk of a taxi that stopped to help. The car took off at speed and I kicked to one side the leg that was left on the street.

When you see so many dead and so many body parts, when you hold them and feel them carefully, you feel their weight, warmth, smell, moisture and you realise that a dead man is just an object. An object that will soon start to stink and become the source of all sorts of dangerous diseases so that it needs to be disposed of and buried as soon as possible. Regardless of how much you loved that person it does not change the fact that they are now an object without a function. A bunch of useless chemical bonds, meat and bones. Among our peoples there is a common phrase that is the cause of our thousand years-long problems, 'Those are the bones of our great grandfathers'. With a limited vocabulary they repeat this phrase as a justification for persecution, killings and rape. I am certain they take it literally because in that bunch of incorrectly joined synapses, there is no space for a deeper metaphor. Bones are: proteins, water, calcium, and few more chemical elements, so please don't kill yourselves over them.

* * *

Once, as I was passing by an old graveyard, I saw a tombstone on an old family tomb destroyed by a mortar round because the Orthodox shelled graveyards during funerals to kill as many as possible.

I came closer and saw that the coffins inside were broken and bones were scattered around the tomb. I grabbed a skull and took it home. I wanted to save it from the strays that would chew on it. I thought of giving it some purpose by making it into a lamp or an ashtray.

When my grandfather saw I brought a human skull home, he simply said, "What a jerk!", took it and threw it in the rubbish. Calcium!

* * *

When I die I want to be cremated and my ashes flushed down the toilet. Fuck calcium. It shouldn't be assigned any greater importance than any other chemical element.

* * *

One night I went to a concert...

It may sound crazy but although there was a war in Sarajevo, there were plenty of concerts, exhibitions and plays. Cultural life was much better than now.

...I stood at the bar and ordered a rice beer. Some guys were playing instrumental music. The drummer Migula, was a guy I had played with since the second year in primary school. He called me up to to the stage to sing something. I got up, took the mic and we started playing together. This became the heavy metal band Almanac.

My music was jazz-rock from an early age. I loved listening to Al Di Meola, Stanley Clarke, Pastorius, Corea, White, Gadd and suchlike characters. And as far as heavy metal is concerned, I like Iron Maiden, I can't say I liked it more that jazz-rock but if you had asked me who I would most like to meet, I'd most certainly reply: Bruce Dickinson, Iron Maiden's front man, because besides being the strongest vocalist on the planet, the man is a pilot. Can anyone be anything more than that? The song Flight of Icarus was my anthem. On 14 December 1994 he played a concert with his band in Sarajevo in the midst of the war. And guess who was his opening act? Us! It sounded surreal. I mean, there was a war on. Who else in their right mind would come to play in the middle of the war?

We hung out that night backstage, Dickinson and myself. We talked about the world of planes that I thought no longer existed. Crazy night.

* * *

After that show, some guy walked up to us and told us that the German Evangelist Church would pay the cost of recording an album in Germany, as we were the best band in Sarajevo. Now that was unreal. We were getting out of the city after three years of shit. It must have been some crazy fucked up joke made by the organiser of this whole fucked up fuck. One day we got a letter of invitation from Germany but it was not easy to get out of Sarajevo. The Blue Road[12] was open but we had to get a whole bunch of documents together before then. We had to have the signature of the president, the supreme military command, the police...

I paused my studies at the Academy and started saying my goodbyes. Those goodbyes were not your usual goodbyes. I was saying goodbye to everyone as if we were to meet again soon when I knew I might be seeing them for the last time. The hardest was saying goodbye to the family. On the one hand, I was glad to be leaving and I know they were glad that I would survive but I couldn't get rid of the thought that I was saving my ass and leaving them in the shit. When we got in the car to leave, everyone was there to wave us off for a long time I am sure. I don't know, I didn't dare look back.

I was off to find Sanja.

* * *

We arrived in Munich late one evening and stayed the night in the Evangelist church. Me and my mates Migula and Sergula the bassist wanted to get some real drugs. So we went out and bought

---

12 The Blue Road was a road under UN protection and the only exit out of the besieged city at the time. It was only open for few months to serve the needs of the UN.

all sorts of things. When the priests came to wake us up in the morning, they found the cross upside down, lines of cocaine across the altar, rolling papers, shit, cans all over the floor and us sleeping in our own vomit on the kneeling cushions. They threw us out and said, "We will do everything we promised but from now on, we want nothing to do with you."

I don't understand why they had got so offended. We were simply craving everything. You know what Chan says? Show me the place on the Earth that is not God, and I will vomit there. Aren't those only objects? Down with the idolatry! This is at the end of the day, the twentieth century for God's sake!

* * *

We took the ICE train to Berlin, where we went on Deutsche Welle TV, performed to playback and told a sad story about the war. The audience nodded in disbelief, cried and applauded.

Our guitarist and keyboard player were staying at a hotel. Meanwhile Sergula, Migula and I, as those responsible for last night, were placed at Jürgen's flat. He was a young junkie quitting heroin who lived in a huge apartment in an attic in Kottbusser Tor. He was loaded with drugs.

The next morning, we were woken by the familiar sound of sniper fire. Before I opened my eyes, I thought I was dreaming it all. And then I opened my eyes and saw we really were in Jürgen's flat. Some nut-job was shooting a sniper rifle from a nearby building. The police special forces soon surrounded and killed him. What a greeting! It was just like home!

Jürgen would get up every few hours, bite off a piece of an apple, draw a line of coke, inhale from a bong and go back to bed. We quickly started feeling at home there. We used his flat as if it was our own. We brought women there and most importantly, used his drugs. Jürgen didn't complain, he'd eat his apple, open the door to a dealer from time to time, pay him, then a smoke, apple, line, sleep.

* * *

After all the crazy fun in Berlin, we went to a studio in a village near Siegen called Hilchenbach, to record the album. In that studio at the far end of the world, I came across my cousin Zoka who was working as an audio engineer. It was utterly unbelievable. The last time I had seen him was when he played in Kotor with his band. He then came there with his motorcycle gang. He was here with his Suzuki GSX750 so two of us would sometimes go to his flat in Hamburg, some 450km away. The studio we were recording in was great for work. The bedrooms were right above it and so if you felt a surge of inspiration at any time, you'd call Zoka who was in the next room to suddenly record a guitar or bass part. We were recording the album for 45 days. We recorded it and then the band split up. All of us went to live in Frankfurt and rented a flat near the Main, all except the guitarist who had found an ex-girlfriend and went to live with her. By then we'd spent all the money we brought with us. Our old friend Kole had been living and working in Frankfurt for a while and he'd sometimes find us illegal jobs in restaurants or on construction sites. The euphoria of freedom was slowly dying away.

* * *

I took the train to a construction site in Heppenheim, about 60km from Frankfurt. As 36 Deutsche Marks was too much to pay for transport, I spent the journey in the toilet. I didn't lock the door, so the engaged sign wouldn't show, which would have been a giveaway. The ticket inspectors would usually catch me somewhere about halfway. They would first knock politely and ask me to come out, then a few of them would come and use force to try to open the door. The toilet was small and if I leaned on the door and place my knee on the opposite wall by the window, there was no chance they could open the door. At first it was a bit tense, but then I got used to it. I'd give up after we'd passed the station just before Heppenheim and they'd throw me off the train just where I wanted to get off. It worked well both there and back.

I had a friend called Belma from Sarajevo in that little place; she was an ex-girlfriend of a singer in a band I used to play in. She worked as a cashier in the local supermarket. In the evening we'd go to Café Zorba, run by a Greek friend of hers. We'd often have Zoran, who was also from Sarajevo, sitting with us. We'd had a few drinks when he started asking me questions about the war. Where was I, what was I doing and so on. It turned out that Zoran and I were actually war comrades. We were on the same frontlines at the same time, just on opposite sides. Maybe it was him I missed that day?

Zoran's wife Branka was dying of bone cancer in a nearby hospital. They had two kids that I met later. That night, Zoran and I sat hugging each other, drunk, stoned, crying. Fuck the war. Fuck it all. We used to be enemies; we are not now.

The two of us remained friends and we still meet up whenever I am in Heppenheim.

* * *

My gang and I put together a new band without a guitarist and we played in Bosnian bars and clubs to survive. Balkan clubs in Germany were distinguished based on religion. Some were frequented by Muslims only, others by Catholics and a third by Orthodox but except for minor differences in lyrics of the songs, there were no other differences among those people. That is where I first saw the true face of our peoples. Our people from rural areas, displaced and made refugees, longing for lamb, cheap alcohol and simple folk music. They were celebrating presidents, religions, nations, criminals and war crimes. Meanwhile hating everyone else, hating us, cursing our Sarajevo mothers and throwing bottles at us.

Why some people from the countryside hates people from the cities that much I will never understand, but the hatred toward people from Sarajevo was always of biblical proportions. At football games, supporters of clubs playing against those from Sarajevo, regardless of the fact that both are Muslim often shout "Fuck Markale!", referring to the horrific massacre at the Sarajevo Markale market where one Orthodox mortar took seventy lives, and wounded over two hundred. While I was in Sarajevo, I never came across such ill-mannered people. A few times I told them all to go fuck themselves, which is also ill-mannered, especially through the microphone. So we had to run, leaving them to enjoy their anti-music performed for them by simple, uneducated village people, the idols of the masses, whose lyrics glorify the nation, religion, the president, criminals and war crimes, or have a cheap erotic edge. Those kinds of acts got paid 4000 – 8000 DM for their stage appearance. They were on stage three times a week, and since they were the favourites of the ruling parties, diplomatic passports enabled them to come and go from the country uninterrupted.

We'd get 50DM. With that money, we ate a doner kebab at the railway station. I'd sometimes go to a phone booth to try to ring Sanja but the machine always said that number was no longer in use. Then we'd go to McDonalds, buy some shit and sit on our balcony, watching the Main, smoking and listening to our album that had no purpose anymore.

Gigs were rare, as were construction jobs. The fines for illegal workers got really high and no one dared to employ us anymore. We were getting more and more depressed.

When I left Sarajevo, I swore to myself that I would never be hungry again, as during the war almost all of us were hungry all the time. I had broken that promise and here I was, hungry again.

We were spending time with two Bosnian seasonal workers, Samir and Legend, great guys who we met at a gig in a nearby bar. They smoked pot as well, so they always brought us the shit but meals got less frequent. We spent a few months on the balcony, totally wasted and mostly hungry. Then the keyboard player and drummer found girlfriends at one of the gigs and went off to live with them. It was just Sergula and myself. We stole a TV and Nintendo from our Serbian neighbours, so we puffed and played Super Mario. Soon the landlord came to visit and since we never paid the rent, he threw us out. It was winter. Sergula and I were on the street, not a dime in our pockets, and without a plan in our heads. We wanted to go to prison for free food so we got on the metro, just riding it stop to stop while thinking what to do. When the ticket inspectors came, we hoped they would take us to prison because we didn't have tickets, but they just threw us off the train and we slept at the station.

It wasn't bad at all at the station. It was warm and you could find lots of cigarette butts that we used to pick and then re-use the tobacco in rolling paper because of hygiene. But later, we'd just take them off the floor and smoke them. We hung out all sorts of lowlifes and homeless, whom we didn't speak German to as we knew only few useful phrases, such as:

– *Wieviel?* – How much?

– *Zwanzig* – Twenty

– *Aber das ist nicht korrektmal, da ist zu Wenig!* – But that's not right, there's too little!

– *Ja, aber das ist auf Maroko* – Yes, but it is from Morocco.

During the day we'd drink beer in front of the shops or in the park and in the evening we'd sleep on benches. When we'd meet someone we knew like Samir or Legend, we'd take a few Marks from them to get something to eat. When we were not hungry the mood was rather different. Nowadays I can say that I enjoyed the gallivanting in a strange way. It was freedom. But we rarely felt full.

We had no clue what was happening in Sarajevo. In a store, few blocks from the station was a TV in a shop window and there was a report on Bosnia on while we were walking past once, about destruction of the Old Bridge in Mostar. I didn't know then that the destruction was ordered by one of the members of my extended family. Some dumbo, ten times removed cousin whom I never met. After he was convicted of war crimes against civilians, he drank poison in the courtroom and died. Naturally, he is a hero to the Catholics. Religions love morons.

We often went to that shop trying to catch more news but MTV was always on, so we'd move on disappointed or we'd stand there in silence, pretending to watch what was happening on the world music scene.

One rainy afternoon, while walking around Frankfurt with Belma, who had come from Heppenheim to bring a letter from my family whom I haven't heard from for months, we noticed a woman's bag on a grey electricity box. I looked around and didn't see anyone. I don't usually put my hand into someone else's bag but I opened this one and saw a bunch of banknotes. A rough estimate would be around ten thousand DM, a wallet with an ID in it, a bank card and the PIN code written on a piece of paper. We didn't think much, we read the address, rang the bell and returned the purse to an old granny. She took the purse and slammed the door in my face. Not even a thank you!

I stood at the door for a long time, just thinking. But because I didn't come up with anything clever, we moved on. How is it possible that you don't get a thank you when you return a purse with money in it? I was thinking of knocking again, the granny would open, I'd take out my nickel-plated Magnum 44 and blow granny's head off, then kill the stroke-paralyzed grandpa in the wheelchair, the two neighbours and a small dog, take the money from the bag and disappear. But I didn't have a nickel-plated Magnum, I love animals and I have a soft spot for the elderly so we just moved on.

"Aren't you going to read the letter?" Belma asked.

"Tonight," I said.

I was squeezing the letter in my pocket the whole day, as if someone were about to take it from me. I wasn't sure if I wanted to open it at all. I wasn't sure what I'd find in there. Are they all alive and in one piece? Judging the handwriting on the envelope I concluded that my mother was alive. Or at least had been a few days earlier when she wrote it.

But what about the others? I knew I couldn't read it without a mountain of emotions welling up. I had a knot in my throat the whole day but I didn't want to show Belma what sort of a wuss I could be. After I saw her off at the train station, I sat on the bench, took the wrinkled letter and felt the knot tighten and close up my throat, rushing the blood to my head and I started crying almost out loud, without having read a word. I could not see what was written through the tears so I ran to a nearby bar to wash my face, slapped myself hard across the face few times in front of the mirror, sat on the toilet and started reading.

"Son, I don't have much time to write as I have to post it in five minutes. Maybe it is better like that as I have nothing nice to say. Granny Dušanka, on top of the usual chores, is reading novels on failed societies and perverted princesses and then retells them to me while I am playing solitaire. Optimism has not departed her. She is very happy when we get electricity on the fourth day, she then makes baked beans and cakes. Of course, we have to eat the beans right away so they don't spoil but the cakes can last us until the next electricity turn-on. Grandpa Milan, as always, does nothing but lie down. To everyone it seems he is just passing time but he tries to convince us he is actually deep in thought. Eni is trying to study, but I am not sure she is succeeding. It seems she is not

as happy as she usually is. It must be because she spends a lot of time in the shelter.

Radenko, same as usual. His working shifts are now 12 hours on, 12 hours off, 12 on, 8 off, 12 on, 6 off and then 24 hours on. Admit it, you've forgotten what that means! Mustafa as usual, is trying different businesses. I haven't seen anyone from your gang because only those who have to move around the city. There are no plays at the theatre, the markets are closed, everything is shut due to security reasons. Grandpa Avdaga and Rabija are in the same position you left them in. Amina, Ema and Zina got missed by a mortar by merely a metre, other than that they are all fine and well. Zora's son got hit by an explosive bullet in the stomach. He's had four surgeries; they've patched up his intestines and his artery and taken out a kidney. He looks like a skeleton in a leather case, but otherwise he is OK. My love, as you can see the atmosphere is very inspirational for living and working. I will soon complete the work on the hotel (we already have ten reservations). I am constantly patching up the holes as we get new ones all the time. I don't have to tell you I am getting recommendations from all sides, which I had naturally expected in all my modesty but I don't feel terribly happy because of that. Only the news of you make me happy. The other night I dreamt that you came back. I woke up soaked in sweat. My love, there, I've told you everything (by the big new candle). I'd love for you to write in detail (although I know you don't like details). How are you? How's your place? How do you spend your time? They are here to get the letter now. Everyone sends their greetings. Love and kisses, Mother!"

My place? My place is great! Everything is great!

I didn't reply to the letter. I couldn't lie. They had somewhat higher expectations for me.

When I told him about the money, Sergula went crazy and didn't speak to me for days. But then we often didn't speak for days, maybe months. We couldn't say anything due to hunger and our inability to change anything. Infirmity was constant; there is no worse feeling in life. Sergula was right, I should have taken at least enough money that we could have had a decent meal and buy a pack of cigarettes each. Not even saying we could have started a new life, found a place, got a haircut, a shave and a bath. If I had given the bag to the police, we would have got 10% of everything. But it was too late for that. The bagful of money situation got us further depressed. I thought a man couldn't be much more fucked up than we were then. It was hard to think that the real shit in life had not even started yet.

* * *

A few months later Samir introduced me to Betty. She was a good looking Italian blonde that I sometimes used to see near the station. I noticed she was always looking at me and she'd smile at me in passing. I never smiled back, thinking she was smiling because of the misery I was in.

Betty was dating Angelo, a man who was supplying coke to whole of western Europe. A big shot.

A first hand man. Betty's job since she was thirteen was to weigh the coke, pack it into envelopes and deliver to different addresses. One day she asked us if we'd like to live in her friend Sanela's flat. So we took our belongings from the station and moved into an apartment in the centre of Frankfurt. For the first few days in the flat I felt weird, contained. It was as if I'd lost something important, as if I had betrayed my homeless comrades that I never even spoke to. My sight was used to wide open space and now it was somehow contained and closed. And it was dark. What have I done? I've exchanged freedom for a flat?

But I quickly got used to it.

There was no power in the flat, so the two of us with experience from the war stole electricity with cables from our neighbours. Then they found out and we almost got locked up. But we didn't feel like going to prison. We liked it there. Other than living under the candlelight like in the war, it wasn't that bad. We were constantly drugged up and hungry. I don't mean the hunger that people feel before breakfast or during fasting but permanently. I was seriously thinking of eating Sergula. It's funny now. It wasn't funny then.

* * *

The flat was frequented by the darkest of characters in the city. Mostly dealers, junkies, killers, Turks,

Moroccans, Albanians, Italians, Polish and Turkish whores, a few lost Bosnians, like the Mostar guy Duca; Sanela's boyfriend or our old friends Samir and Legend. And Pit Bull, a quiet guy the spitting image of a Pit Bull, with a nasty scar on his forehead. When he was fifteen, he had ended up in an Orthodox concentration camp with his family. Him and his father were forced to perform fellatio on one another, while the Orthodox were watching and killing themselves laughing. Then they got a bullet each in the back of the head. Both him and his father. He miraculously survived. I really didn't want to hear that story, but he told it to me and I don't know why.

Then Robby, a crazy Italian who lost a ring together with a finger on a barbed wire fence, while running away from the police carrying drugs. He was Angelo's right hand.

* * *

Samir came one day and said his girlfriend was pregnant and that they were leaving to go live in Berlin. He brought a doner kebab for me and Segula, we lit up a spliff, kissed and said goodbye. Legend just disappeared. Months later, we heard he shot some Turk and ran away, then went to the hospital and burst into the surgery while they were operating on the guy, fighting for his life and emptied the magazines of both pistols into the poor sod. He got eight years. I often imagine this scene. Legend bursting in through the two-leaf door into the operating theatre and in slow motion taking out two pistols out from under a leather coat and shooting the guy on the operating table, while the doctors throw themselves on the floor. He never wore a leather coat. It's only me imagining him like that but he did carry two pistols. Fuck, I haven't seen that even in a movie. It is a kind of scene that deserves to be shot.

* * *

On Saturdays we had LSD seances. Twenty or so people sat around a candle and two experienced gurus taking us through different trips and everyone imagining and seeing the same thing. Except Duca, LSD did nothing to him. Every time he'd get really keen and wait for something to happen, something to hit him, and the only thing that happened was the waiting.

The other days we'd hit up with anything and everything. Mostly coke as it was there in kilos, weed, hashish and me heroin sometimes. OK, crack a few times as well.

* * *

WARNING: IF YOU HAVE TO MESS WITH DRUGS, STAY AWAY FROM HEROIN AND CRACK!

* * *

Betty and I were in a secret relationship for a while already. We hid as much as we could but with time we got careless and relaxed so Angelo found out about us. Some very dangerous people were looking for us so we ran to Hamburg, to my cousin Zoka's. Sanela told us that Angelo's people had been looking for us, that they were in the flat and bashed up everything with baseball bats, and that they would find us for sure anywhere we hid. Five or six days later we ran out of coke and returned to Frankfurt. I hid at Kole's and Betty with her folk out of the city. One night, Kole and I sat down with a guitar and got wasted with alcohol and drugs. I woke up on a bus on the Austrian border with the guitar next to me. I searched my pockets and found a passport, 100DM and ticket to Sarajevo. So it seemed I was going back home.

* * *

I will never forget the look on my mother's face when she saw me get out of the lift in the hallway in front of the flat. Throughout this time, we had spoken maybe five times. She, as well as I, didn't know I was coming. We both cried.

* * *

The war had stopped in Sarajevo few months earlier but the situation was pitiful. People, similar to those that threw bottles at me and cursed my Sarajevo mother, had their grip over everything: the judiciary, the health service, the police, the state, everything! And they still do.

* * *

I went to Kotor to find Sanja. For a long time I was under no illusion. I just wanted to see her and make sure everything was OK. On the main square near the courtroom, while I was in a phone booth trying to call her, dialling a number that the new owner of her restaurant gave me, I saw her walk past me with a husband and a two-year old daughter in a pram. I dropped the handset. Our eyes met and after such a long time, at the same time we both said probably the dumbest "Ciao" anyone could say. She hadn't changed a bit. I met her husband, stroked her daughter on the head and that was it.

"See you!" I said. While I was watching her leave, I knelt on the sidewalk, as if I was looking for something and I cried like a baby there in the middle of the main square, in front of a thousand people. I cried because of everything but mostly because of happiness, I think. I saw her happy and that was the most precious thing to me. Now back to reality.

* * *

I told Betty I was in Sarajevo and she came a week later. We didn't have money to rent a place so we searched the ads in papers, looking for the cheapest room. We found it, went to the address and rang the bell. A fifty-year-old paraplegic called Duško opened the door.

"Hi, we are here for the room."

"Yes, yes, please come in. My daughter Mirna is letting her room. She is travelling to Belgium for a month for a workshop. Come in and have a look, she'll be here soon.

It was a high ceilinged Austro-Hungarian flat, our room was around 15 square metres with a shared toilet and kitchen, no TV and no radio but never mind, it was 150 Marks a month. Perfect.

Mirna came round early in the evening in a white robe, holding a white cat in her arms. She was trying to be strict but she was anything but that. Like a mobster in a B-rated crime movie, with the cat she was stroking. It was surreal. With a very serious expression on her face, she said:

"Just so you know, no messing about, no friends, no loud music and no drinking till late at night. Is that clear?"

She was dead cute. I fell in love, right there and then. I said:

"OK, we won't stay long just until we sort ourselves out. What do you do?"

"I study acting, second year."

"Amazing, we will be in the same class then!"

She was as glad as I was but she tried to hide it from Betty, who saw it all clearly right away but pretended not to.

I made friends with Duško. We used glass paint to draw mosques on empty alcohol bottles and sold them to foreigners on the street. That's how we earned enough to buy a bottle of vodka or wine. Sometimes an extremist would come up to us and tell us we couldn't draw mosques on liquor bottles. There were times when it was rather tense but they usually stayed away because Duško was in a wheelchair. Betty's relationship got colder with me over time. She decided to go back to Germany and I helped her make that decision. She later married Angelo. Then divorced him.

* * *

Downtown, I saw my good friend Krepo who I used to hang around before the war and who I tried to get out of the army, at least for a while, by advising him to feign insanity and be taken to the nuthouse. He didn't succeed in getting into the psychiatric hospital but he did spend some time at neuropsychiatry and that spared him few nasty battles. After a brief chat he said:

"What do you think we hit up some heroin?"

"Of course! Heroin is like flying!"

We went to see his cousin, a dealer called Dimension. We hit up and life was great.

Krepo and I always used drugs for contemplating. We had similar life philosophies and had no limits in it all. We later fixed up ourselves with cocaine, then weed, then parcopas, hash, LSD, ecstasy, Akineton, Artane, downing it all with rakija and beer. It was Krepo's favorite mix and I wasn't complaining!

* * *

A few days after the classes started, Mirna and I started dating and it was great but I was spending more and more time with Krepo and Dimension.

* * *

Dimension was a good mate but fuck, he was a nutter. He was a two metres tall muscly guy, tattooed all over with a shaven head and a huge baseball bat-induced scar across the middle of his head. By that time, he'd already done time for one murder and nobody knew about the other one in Zagreb. Once he shot at his sister and parents with an automatic rifle. They only survived by throwing themselves on the floor. His cat survived as well, when he threw her from the fifth-floor window. Her balance was a bit off after that. He liked throwing things off heights. Fire extinguishers, for example. He used to throw them at parked cars from tall buildings. When an extinguisher falls from, let's say the seventeenth floor onto a car, it almost folds it in two. Such things brought great joy to him. He would often use a spoon to eat the aquarium fish feed but I couldn't work out whether he ate the crushed dried insects to be cool or if he really liked them. Other than being crazy, he was also a computer genius and worked on IT system maintenance in the OHR (Office of the High Representative) and knew all their top secret information, which wasn't particularly interesting then nor worth a mention now.

* * *

Since I didn't have the money to buy heroin every day, I started dealing it with Dimension. We were petty dealers, last hand men, conmen basically. We often sold scraped off façade from buildings and even more often, pure sugar to our customers. We had a few regulars that we called diabetics. Kerim for example, a guy who ran a nearby bar, would buy sugar from us every day. I'd take a small package of sugar from the coffee machine right in front of him, go to the toilet, crush it up with a card, pack it in aluminum foil, give him the package and take 20 Marks from him. We'd then use that to buy real Horse[13] and hit up. This was sometimes repeated two, three or four times a day. He was our favourite customer and the only junkie putting on weight by shooting up 'heroin'. The best was that after a year of taking pure sugar, Kerim decided to go to a commune for rehab and spent five years there, without ever having tried real junk.

The commune is a Catholic Church institution with a rehab program for drug and other addictions. The addicts are treated with occupational therapy. The commune produces its own food, so the addicts work with crops and cattle. In the rest of their 'free' time they make souvenirs which they later sell in Medjugorje, a small town in Herzegovina which is a Catholic pilgrimage site where the Virgin Mary allegedly appeared some 40.000 times. The commune earns 8.5 million Euro annually for the church from selling these souvenirs. TAX FREE!

---

13 Heroin

* * *

We had a cool thing going when we were out of money for drugs, which was very often, to buy newspapers, open the obituaries page and look for people who died after "a short and serious illness". We'd go to the address published by the family so that people could come and show their respects, we'd show up at the door and say that we are brothers whose mother was dying of cancer, and if there was any pain medication left, could they give it to us. Sometimes we'd get ordinary pain killers, sometimes they'd send us off with a few swear words and often they'd give us pure morphine, which was like a holiday for us. We liked morphine the best.

We had a guy in Travnik, a small city in Bosnia, who worked in the UN field hospital and who took litres and litres of morphine off the base. He sold us ampules for 20 Marks each but he was hooked on it as well, so the price varied depending on how much he needed it. It could be anywhere from 20 to 50 Marks. The army eventually figured out that 'Miss Emma' was going missing, so they stopped the shipments. He then sold us some other shit in ampules that made us feel like someone had smacked us across the face. It was like a failed attempt at morphine rehab.

* * *

Mirna knew I was using and few times she injected me with heroin when I was so bad I couldn't do it myself. She didn't like all that but she loved me. I loved her a lot as well but sometimes I could be a right prick, especially when I was in a crisis. Which was happening more and more. She got pregnant. I talked her into an abortion.

* * *

I remember my first overdose. Actually, I don't remember it. I remember the before and the after. My mate Šaks called me at about three in the morning to come to our mate's workplace. Žuti worked as a night guard in a company next to my building. The two of them sat on a radiator at the reception of Elektroprivreda and they let me sit on an armchair so I could hit up with the latest stuff Žuti got. I cooked up the smack, drew the syringe, stuck the needle in and while we were talking about non-related stuff, I quickly ran the content of the syringe into the vein. Suddenly, it was as if someone had used the remote to change the channel. I saw the two of them upside down, off the floor, on the same spot, completely white and I felt my tongue hurting really badly.

"What was that?", I asked in shock, barely uttering the words as my tongue was swollen and painful.

"Fuck you, you are alive!"

"I don't get it, what happened?"

"You've been dead for twenty minutes. We carried you upstairs to the toilet, splashed water on you, used the safety pin to pull your tongue out, pushed salt in your vein, slapped you and when we realised you were dead-dead, we brought you back to the reception and started discussing how and what with to dismember you and where to we throw away your body parts, so Žuti wouldn't lose his job."

If people tell you that when you die you see a tunnel of light and fields of flowers, don't believe a single fucking word. They are either lying, like when they were children, or their brain was still somewhat functioning and was able to create such images for them.

There were many more overdoses. I don't know the exact number but the number of fields of flowers and tunnels is zero.

Žuti checked out using the same stuff day or two later but he did not come back. He threw the spoon away, as we junkies say in professional jargon. He was a good mate. Lots of good mates left during those years.

Faruk. What a great guy. I remember years before, him, Edin and me stole his dad's brand-new Mercedes from the garage every night. When the old man fell asleep, Faruk would nick the keys and we'd push the car all the way to the end of the street and start it then, so the old man didn't hear the sound of the engine. We'd return it in the morning, few minutes before the old man woke up to go to work in the same car.

"Good morning kids, how are you?", he'd say.

"Morning Uncle Hajder, have you had a good night's sleep?", was our reply, barely restraining ourselves from bursting out laughing.

Faruk was doing some dodgy business with cheques around then, so we were always loaded. It was a time of great devaluation in the currency and by the time the cheque was cashed its value was at least ten times lower. Banknotes with more and more zeroes were printed daily. One night we went to the Hotel Bristol night club, so Faruk could lose his virginity. Hotel room 300 DM, hooker for half an hour 300 DM, some cocktail she was drinking 300 DM, arrangements with the waiter etc. But the money was no issue. The hookers liked us so much that during their free time, when they weren't too exhausted from the night before, we started hanging out. Girls from Zrenjanin in Serbia, Zorana and Violeta. We used to cheer them during their striptease acts.

On one perfect day, while having coffee in some garden of a coffee shop, Faruk took a magazine from the next table and started flipping through the car adverts. His face lit up when he saw the photo of tornado red Buggy. It had a 1600cc Volkswagen Beetle engine, a folding roof and a black roll-bar. Eight nickel-plated exhaust pipes were sticking out from the back. It had alloy wheels, wide tires and Recaro seats. It was 13,000DM. We went to the bank, cashed some cheques and went to the near-by town to get the car. We didn't haggle. It looked mean so we named it Red Death. Three of us rode through town in the Buggy, with three open um-brellas in an unbelievable rainstorm. It was worth it for the looks of people on trams and trolley-bus-es looking at us, pointing and laughing. But at that moment, there was no one that even came close to us. We were larger than life.

The war found Faruk at his summer house, near the city. He was killed by some Catholics in front of his house, in front of his parents. They killed him so they could take his buggy. Who could have known that when we were reading the car ads, that on that day, we were buying his death. Edin told me later that when it happened, his mother pushed him around, dead, in a wheelbarrow for days, screaming.

* * *

Then Schwarz. He beat me up twice in primary school, but we got on well later on. He was the state judo champion. Although he practiced on me, I

99

won't take all the credit. He lost both his legs in the war. Above the knee amputations. He lived two floors up from Mirna. He had a big pit bull that pulled his wheelchair and helped him up the stairs. One evening my friends and I saw him in the park selling his dog to some guy and I told them that Schwarz might have decided to kill himself.

That night he died of the 'golden hit' – suicide by overdose.

My mate Rizo, who right in front of me took off his mother's golden earrings while she was sleeping on a couch in the living room so he could buy sugar with a bit of heroin from me; also dead! Brain cancer.

Deba, the guy who worked in the grill and from whom, with a hamburger, you could also get a packet of heroin or marijuana; dead. He threw away the spoon.

Bakir, a childhood friend who had a motorcycle we all admired him for. A blue *MZ 250*. He could barely get through a single day without getting into a fight with at least three guys. Dead. He threw away the spoon.

Zlako, a dealer and a good guy when he wasn't high, which was practically never. He threw away the spoon.

Željko, a stuntman. Died while working on a movie stunt.

Miki. Hung himself during a heroin withdrawal.

Cinci and Čopelj, two of the only punks at the time. Best friends since childhood. Died on the same day at two different locations. Mortar fire.

Boki. Don't know what happened to him. It must have been the spoon.

Bugi, a guitarist, he threw away the spoon.

Mario, a tenor of Sarajevo Opera. We played gigs together in bars before the war. Sniper.

Sanel checked out the first time he tried heroin. A good lad. I knew his whole family and protected him like a brother. I never let him try Horse but he found someone who did.

Irfan. Shot in the head with an anti-aircraft machine gun bullet and hit a pole with his car on the first day of the war. Two of his friends got killed with him.

Aco. My professor of acting. Hell of a guy. Cancer.

Marko. The drummer in one of my bands. Cancer.

Ćuta, he once tattooed me and I paid him with heroin. The spoon.

Keva. Traffic accident.

Roman. Got a job in a sawmill and was high when he fell into the wood-cutting machine.

Bojan. A class colleague. Suffocated during an epileptic fit in his sleep.

Žan. One of the best and funniest actors I ever met. Cancer.

Tanja. Jumped off the balcony in her flat on the third floor. She was holding a half-smoked cigarette in her hand.

Suvad. Bullet.

Linda. Hung herself.

Hare. Sniper.

Maja. Pills.

Miksi. Carbon monoxide. Miksi. My Miksi.

Yes, Dimension's grandmother was also dead. She was hit by a car on the pedestrian crossing near the National Theatre. Upset by it all, he got in a car and ran over the first old woman he came across. The poor woman died on the way to the hospital and he got 22 months' imprisonment because his attorney convinced the judge it was accidental.

I sometimes used to take him drugs to the prison. I packed heroin and ecstasy in condoms, put them in milk and then glued the carton with superglue. I'd then give it to his mother on the way in, to take the milk together with some homemade cookies. Cookies and milk. It makes sense and is less suspicious.

After a year of good behavior, he got transferred to a semi-open prison on Mount Igman, near Sarajevo. Iggy and I organised his escape. Actually, we just picked him up in a car at the agreed time and place.

It may sound a bit weird that a convict on the run hides in his own flat but it took the police a month to find him there. I guess they thought he wouldn't be that crazy. They didn't extend his sentence, they just cut his privileges and returned him to the old prison. He didn't rat on us, so we were in the clear.

I met him not long ago. He was walking around the city with two bags full of weapons. He had just got out of prison. He did six years for some guy whom he and his girlfriend kept dead in the closet for a week until he got very smelly.

* * *

In the meantime, Šaks and I were dealing heroin and Iggy and I were dealing weed. We bought the weed in Mostar in kilos and because all the other weed dealers got arrested, we were the only ones and we held the market, dictating the price. Our packets were ridiculously small, and we were always criticised by Iggy's parents who helped make the packets up with us.

"You are insane! You should be ashamed of yourselves for selling such small packets," they used to say. "Someone will kill you over this!"

Some of our customers used to tell us that when they opened the packet, they didn't know where the weed was or that you'd get more cocaine for the same money. But greed did its thing and we were doing well for a while.

Out of the money made we'd buy Horse that Šaks and I mixed with sugar and sold again. We were once caught on the boundary line with Republika Srpska near Sarajevo, where the heroin was often sold. We were in withdrawal and we bought a lot of heroin for all the money we had. We went into a derelict house to get high, and I had just pulled the liquid into the syringe when I heard footsteps behind the wall. I quickly put the loaded syringe into my left sock. In my right sock I had 13 packets of heroin and another half a packet in the small drug pocket in my jeans. Two plain clothes police-men approached us and took everything from Šaks right away. A police van arrived, they put us in it and drove us to the station. A policeman frisked me and soon found the packets in my right sock.

"Do you have any more?"

"Well, fuck it, I don't. You found it all!"

"And what's this?" he asked while taking out the packet from my jeans.

"That is another half and there is no more. That's it. May I use the toilet?" I asked.

"Why? Do you have more drugs? You think you can throw it away so we don't find it, ha-ha-ha?

"Yes, ha-ha-ha. No, I want to do a hit, ha-ha-ha. No, really, I need to piss!"

"You may, but an officer will go with you."

We went to the toilet and the policeman stood by the open door and watched me. I started pissing so out of decency, he turned his head. As he did so, I somehow managed to get the syringe from the sock and I hit up right in the police station. I left the syringe on the cistern. Šaks went nuts when I returned to sit on the bench, high as a kite. He could not believe it. I managed to convince the police that I wasn't a dealer and that I bought the drugs for my own use, so I just paid a 60 Mark fine for possession.

* * *

That year, Šaks, Iggy, Mirna and myself, together with some other friends, decided to celebrate New Year's on Jahorina, Olympic mountain held by the Orthodox.

This wasn't the smartest idea as the war had just ended and Jahorina was still a stronghold of the Army of Republika Srpska, but I wanted to see those people. I wanted to see what a person who can shell a maternity hospital looks like. I was truly intrigued. The house where we planned to celebrate was an army-rented place. When we went there few days before the celebration to make arrangements, we sat with them in a bar. Iggy and I with the senior military officers.

"Where are you from?", the fat general asked.

"From Sarajevo!"

"Which Sarajevo? Serb or Muslim?"

Iggy kicked me gently on the shin under the table, trying to tell me that this was neither the time nor the place for truth.

"Muslim."

A few of the officers immediately stood away from the table and Iggy went all green and started scratching his forehead to hide the eyebrows he was using to covertly give me signals to stop any further talk about my wartime engagement.

"And were you in the army?"

Fuck it, the question was too direct and came out of nowhere.

"Ah well, of course I was in the army. Everyone was in the army!"

Iggy hit my shin with his Dr Martens boot so hard that I immediately felt the blood dripping down my leg and I nearly howled. He knew who we were sitting with.

"Why?" the general asked.

"Why? Well, because I hated you. I spent hours and hours staring through the sniper sights, waiting for one of you so I could split your skull open in cold blood. That is how much I hated you. I thought I was fighting for the Bosnia Herzegovina that they promised us. A single secular state, the country of all peoples and nationalities and all its citizens. I was young and stupid and as such, I was cunningly manipulated and used by a small, but despicable circle of rich men with a totally different ambition. Used much like yourself..."

* * *

Even though the Bosnia and Herzegovina is officially divided into two parts, in real life it is de-
vided in three parts on religious grounds. In the
Muslim part, the then-president brought his family and their friends to power; mostly unqualified
and semi-literate people, who saw the running of
the state as their private family business. For example, his son who later also became president,
today owns banks, hotels, gas stations and shopping centres. And the court system is designed so
that, from the beginning of the war until today
none of the politicians were tried for corruption
or misuse of position, although during the war
nearly $10,000,000,000 (yes, you are reading it cor-
rectly, ten billion US Dollars) of different foreign
donations disappeared. That was the third big 'job'.
International donations were made after the war
as well, for reconciliation, for families to return
to their homes, for refugees and the displaced and
for agriculture. "The booty" was split between the
different religious communities and organisations
that were accomplices to the ruling nationalist parties and never came across the common people
who were in primary need of them.

The fourth and the biggest 'job' of the ruling
party was the 'Privatisation' of property previously owned by the state. It was all about giving

ex-soldiers, for each month spent at war, a certificate to the value of 400 DM. Since there was no means of cashing those bonds, people from the ruling party bought off the certificates for 3% of their value and then sold all the state property to themselves, also for a miserable price. The state got useless pieces of paper and they got all the available property, for a maximum of 3% of its real worth.

* * *

"...but luckily I never killed anyone and I'm really pleased about that. I hope that's not a reason not to have something to drink. Waiter!"

"Kudos to you lad!" he said, after a long break. "If you need anything, just say so. I though all you Turks were shits."

"There must be some mistake. We are not Turks. Turks wear a moustache and have big knives for doner kebabs!"

It was as I thought it would be. I met ordinary people. They didn't have sharpened, bloody canines, nor bloodshot popped-out eyes. There were manipulated, small people.

* * *

The Republika Srpska Army guarded our house for the New Year, just to make sure no one spoiled the fun for us. The general himself came to wish me a Happy New Year and to invite me to come in thirteen days' time, to celebrate the Orthodox New Year with them, and said that he intended to introduce me to his soldiers as the enemy soldier who had the balls to come and talk to him like that. I went and it was all OK.

* * *

Šaks went to Italy right after the New Year. He got caught on the border due to some robbery he did a few years back and he ended up in prison. He got a year and a half. Fuck it Šaks, change your vocation!

His sister Su, also a junkie, brought me a letter from him. He said he was doing fine, that he has a good gang, no lack of drugs. His cellmate said hello, he was doing life. He robbed some guy, then put him in the trunk and lit the car up. The guy was all burnt in the car for three days and guess what? He survived and then later testified against him. Fuck it, Šaks, seems you are in bad company again.

* * *

Iggy left to Serbia to sort out some alimony paperwork, but was caught on the border for a computer theft he did few years back, and he was sent to prison for few months too.

Su and I decided to turn her mate Zlaja, a top athlete and young hope for BiH in snowboarding, into a junkie and rip off his money. No one could match my skill in praising heroin and Zlaja turned into a junkie.

We went one day to his flat to get high. On the way to his room, we said hello to his parents sitting on the couch, their back turned to us, watching TV. "Hello kids!" they said over their shoulders.

The goods I bought from Šile in the Orthodox region, were well known as the worst there was. You needed to take at least half a gram to feel anything but most of the dealers were locked up by now, so there wasn't really a choice. We bought a gram, split it in three, cooked it up and loaded three syringes. Su's veins weren't too good, so it was difficult for her to inject. She went to the toilet to spare us from looking at the massacre. Zlaja and I injected in his room. I got hit by a terrible flash and when I opened my eyes, I saw Zlaja in his armchair, dead. I came to and started reviving him but it wasn't working. Why wasn't Su helping me? Then I realised; she must be dead in the toilet. I went to check and found her lying by the toilet seat. A dead weight is not easy to pick up but somehow I managed and took her out of the toilet in total silence so the parents didn't turn around. As usual, they had no idea that their child was using. I brought her into the room and put her down on the floor. Do I try saving Zlaja or Su? I'll save Zlaja, it is his flat at the end of the day. After God knows how long, Zlaja showed signs of life. I slapped him two more times, hard and he came about.

"What happened?"

"I'll explain later. Save Su!" I said to him, totally exhausted.

And Su came about. That was a close call!

* * *

Zlaja freaked out and quit heroin. He went back to sports but never with the same enthusiasm again. Su went to the commune in Medjugorje. She spent seven years there and became a missionary. After prison, Šaks went to a commune in Italy.

* * *

Duca came back from Germany and asked me to come to Mostar and be the best man at his wedding. I called the Chamber Theatre right away to lend me a suit from one of the plays to wear at the wedding and bought 5 grams from Šile for the trip. Duca and Selma greeted me in a Lincoln stretch limo and took me to the municipality to finalise the paperwork and official parts. We spent the day driving around and drinking and by the time the wedding was to begin, I was done. At 8pm, I went up to the hotel room, took another hit and fell asleep. He never forgave me for this. My phone woke me in the morning, a 'colleague' asking if I have a connection for heroin as it seems Šile had got busted as well. He was my last option. What now? Everyone had got busted. There was no more heroin in Sarajevo. I got on the bus and took off to Croatia to get the stuff and arrange a permanent supply.

* * *

I knew a few guys in Croatia and Montenegro who were working with somewhat larger amounts. I used to bring 50 – 200 grams from there, often in body cavities. I packed heroin into small 5-gram balls and put them in a condom and then, excuse my French, up my ass. Fuck it, no one wants to go to prison. Once the condom broke in there but luckily the balls didn't disintegrate, otherwise I would have died but it was a pain in the ass getting it all out of there. Use your imagination.

Once I carried 50 grams in one lump, from Podgorica, Montenegro to Ulcinj. It was a biggish ball, wrapped in aluminium foil, about the size of a tennis ball. I carried that one in my hand, not where you thought.

Just as I was about to get out of the car on the beach where we arranged to meet, we got surrounded by several police officers from the narcotics squad. I thought that was it. As I got out of the car, I used the hand that I was holding the heroin in to grab the handle above the door, the one usually used to hang jackets on, and noticed that it had a built-in spring that returns the handle to the starting position. I put the heroin there and the handle pressed it up so it didn't fall down. While four policemen were taking the car apart another two were interrogating me. But as usual in those situations, I was cool as if nothing was happening.

My philosophy was that whatever happens one day I will laugh at it. So, if I'll be able to laugh about it one day, why not start laughing right away instead of panicking ahead of time? If they find the drugs, I'll adjust to the situation, but they need to find them first. These tactics worked every time and I never got caught. Well, almost never.

The heroin, right there under their noses the whole time, was not found.

* * *

In Split, Croatia, I had a dealer called Frane who carried drugs across the border in a wooden leg purpose-built for these things. Once they found a kilo of Horse in it, so he went down for two years and then he changed his strategy. He had lost his leg in a car accident when, while he was riding a bike, a Fićo[14] hit his side. It was in the eighties.

Frane's stuff was 70% heroin and was so strong that it caused hallucinations. Sarajevo heroin was only 1-3% pure and 50 grams of this stuff in Sarajevo would result in half a kilo of the strongest Horse in town. I bought 50 grams and planned to take the ferry to Dubrovnik with my mate Siniša, mix the stuff there, sell one part so we have money to stay for a while and then bring the rest home. Frane packed it all up in one big aluminium foil packet. It was a dark night and we went to the beach to get high and wait for the morning and the ferry. We had enough money for tickets only.

"I am so done, I can't even see what I am hallucinating," Sina said then fell off the bench and remained laying on the floor.

We were soon joined by a girl called Maja and as any guy who was well brought up would, I offered her a line to snort.

"Yes, please!" she said cheerfully.

"OK, just hold the lighter so I can unwrap the packet."

While I was slowly unwrapping the foil, the plastic lighter in her hand overheated and just as I opened up the foil, Maja got burnt and waved her

---

14 Fićo – A car made in Yugoslavia Zastava 750 – based on the Fiat 600.

hand spilling our 50 grams over the fine sand on the beach in the night. Silence.

A few minutes of utter silence. Only the light breeze could be heard. The same breeze was moving our heroin over the whole of Croatia. Our plans for the future fell through. Fell through the grains of sand.

We started eating the sand. We shoved it in our mouths and nearly suffocated but the heroin flew with the wind into the night. Maja just disappeared and the two of us licked the aluminum foil, hoping some heroin was stuck in the creases and waited for the most fucked up sunrise in our lives. What now? We only have the money for the ticket and because the trip to Dubrovnik fell through for justifiable reasons, we now have to buy a ticket to Sarajevo. If we buy some stuff, just to get better, we won't even have money for the ticket to Sarajevo, and there we have nowhere to buy heroin, as everyone dealing got busted. Such a shitty situation if there ever was one. Setting off towards Sarajevo, suffering withdrawal the whole of the trip, then being in withdrawal for the next few days at home and getting off the heroin simply wasn't an option. Siniša remembered he had some relatives in Split and he took off. I was left on my own and I didn't even have a lighter any more to light a cigarette. The light was slowly coming up on the left side and was diffusely lighting up the sky. *The heroin is coming down, I'll soon need more. The sun is too slow in coming out. Time is dragging slowly.* The scene itself, usually perfect, seemed like an overly ambitious attempt of an amateur artist to paint the scenery in oil paint on the canvas that would, in the best case scenario, end up on the wall of a stinky room in a cheap roadside hotel and it seemed to me if I vomited the scene colouring would be prettier. It was a clear sign of an abstinence symptom.

The beach was getting busy, children were making faces and running in front of me as they ran to get into the sea, splashing each other and every drop that accidentally hit me hurt. My skin is freezing and burning at the same time. Oh how I hate their carelessness joy and lack of care for people in withdrawal on the beach. And in my head, like hundred times before, the same question: "Will this ever stop? Is it possible I can't do better than this?". I just want to be a pilot! I want to fly! Speaking of flying, I have to call Frane and ask him to lend me some goods so I can pull myself through but I can't call him too early so he doesn't wake up grumpy. I have to be patient until 11:00, at least. Since I was a regular, he lent me 10 grams, which I never repaid. Fuck it, he knew I was a junkie.

I got on the bus towards Sarajevo, full of pensioners.

My old trick was to get on the bus, hide heroin somewhere in the back and then sit at the front and if police asked, I'd play dumb. It's not mine.

Since I was in a rush this time, I left the heroin in my bag in the hold, thinking I would move it to the back during the first restaurant stop because we always stopped at the same place on that route. I had a half packet in my wallet to use on the way. When we set off, I made sure nobody could see and snorted it up my nose. All of it, and fell into a coma. I was woken by a customs officer, asking for my passport. He gave me a look, took the passport and got out. I sat by the window and saw him standing next to the bus with the driver, looking at my passport and telling him to open the luggage hold. Shit! I thought how my name was not on the bag and it could then be anyone's but on the bus with fifty pensioners and the air-conditioning on, I was the only one sweating. That was it. It had to happen at some point. The door to the luggage load opened upwards. They opened it right under my window, so I couldn't see what was happening down there. The customs officer, still with my passport in his hand, went to his hut. He was there a long time. Hours it seemed. I already started thinking about what I would tell my folks. I guess I'd have a right to a phone call, like in the movies. He came out again. I was sweating and using my fingers to peel off the wet, sweat-glued T-shirt off my chest, hoping the sweaty mark will be less visible like that or as if I wanted to say, "This is not my T-shirt, I have no idea why it is on me!" In slow motion, he came towards me, looking at me. I was already slowly standing up from my seat, ready to surrender without making too much fuss, he passed all the people and, and, and... gave me my passport back. And then walked off.

"All good. Bon voyage!"

Life is a work of fiction.

* * *

Although I was hooked, the studying was going surprisingly well. I had high grades in vocational subjects and played lots of parts in the theatre. Sometimes high, sometimes in withdrawal, sometimes clean. I got clean a lot of times. Getting clean of heroin was always followed by a creative period, so during one of those I invented a self-rising toilet seat, ideal for the disabled. I invented a hotel version, electric and digital. I went to the patent registry, and just as I was to patent it, I'd get hooked again and realistically, I was too lazy to type up the thirty pages needed for the invention to be patented.

Five or six years later, some guy in Japan patented the invention and became a multimillionaire.

My next invention was an electric power station that would use gravity, air and huge pressure at deep sea levels to produce power, but I was never sure it would really work. I also worked out how to make power plants using sea waves.

These were later built as well.

Then a laser stick for the blind which vibrates when something interrupts the light beam. The intensity of the vibration would reveal the distance to the physical obstacle. This isn't patented either. I am giving the idea away as an act of charity.

Then an electro-plasmatic jet engine for planes that has no consumption. Then a car that has no consumption and has more horsepower than conventional cars. These engines could be used for other transport and for production of electricity. They could fully replace all the engines running on fossil fuel. Those engines would work on... actually... I can't tell you what they would be operating on because then you'd get rich and won't give anything to me. And just as I was starting to draw the outline – I got hooked again.

Mirna was putting up with it all. The noble ideas, patents, drugs, getting clean, all of it. She loved me so much and would just take it all but not cheating. Others cheat but they keep it quiet. I never could. I couldn't even say it was a planned, mean adultery, because I was used up, in a bad mental state, without clear memory of the events but regardless, I was with someone else and my conscience wouldn't let me look her in the eye and pretend nothing had happened. After I told her, she left me and that hit me so hard that it turned my world upside down. As is usually the case, only then did I realise what I have lost. I spoke to her, begged her to forgive me, promised I'd change and quit drugs, but she knew I was lying. And that hurt her more than the fact I cheated on her.

* * *

At 3am I went, drunk, under her window and called her name. Some woman spoke to me from the basement flat. She told me to fuck off because her children were asleep. I told her all sorts of shit and left. Her husband, called Jigibau, came looking for me at the Academy carrying a gun, just as I left to buy Horse. While he was looking for me, his car got stolen. Later that night he went to the arranged place with money to buy his car back from the thieves. They took the money and killed him.

* * *

I lost all the parts I played at the theatre and left the position of teaching assistant at the acting class. In the class where I was running the lessons, we had another junkie. Before the lesson, I'd sell him Horse and then I'd get high with half of his stuff and only then start the lesson.

* * *

It was all shit. Mirna and I would run into each other at bars, we'd hug and cry. She had a few boy-friends after me, nothing too serious but I didn't take it well. I was with lots of girls at that time. I took that much better. I knew I had to get clean for-ever and I was trying but it just wasn't happening.

* * *

I found myself a girlfriend. Alisa was known for being Miss BiH beauty queen for a few days. Then some idiot photographer gave some photos of her to the press. Photos that he took for her portfolio. She was nude in those, so they took the title of Miss Beauty away. They took away the sash, her privacy and her reputation. Just another ugly story among all the other ugly Bosnian stories.

Ćelo, one of the most dangerous guys in the country, wanted to be with her. A point of prestige, I guess.

He was the commander of the wartime military police, that authorised itself to seize property for the 'use of the army' (cars, flats, food, jewellery, money, etc). Towards the end of the war, the po-litical leadership decided to execute him. He got a sniper bullet directly in the heart. And survived! Later he used drug and racketeering money to build a mosque, so they let him be. This was not the only ordered execution. The deputy minister of the interior was relieved of his duties by means of explosives planted under his car. A former Bosnian Army general was also intended to be killed by explosives. Half of his family was killed but he survived. The perpetrators of these crimes were never found.

He was constantly calling her on her mobile, threatening. Once I took the phone from her and told him, "Listen up you monkey, call her one more time, and you'll be dealing with me!", and then I hung up. While I was saying those words, I knew then what kind of shit I was getting myself into. You simply don't talk to Ćelo like that but there was no turning back. Two seconds later, my own phone rang.

"Fedja, is that you? It's Ćelo. I'll fuck your #%+*#%}#!"

I hung up. How did he know my number? This was a problem. A big one.

I borrowed a gun but still we tried not to move about much. Such guys usually send a kid to follow you to your house, then they come and pay a visit... from there, you can use your fucking imagination!

* * *

Iggy and I set off to Mostar to get the usual shipment of weed. Alisa came with us but didn't know we were planning to buy drugs. We used the British

Council's Land Rover with diplomatic plates; Iggy worked there as a driver. Our vehicle was already well known to the Mostar narco-mafia. We parked at the parking lot near the burnt down shopping centre as usual. The unusual bit was that they came in two Audi A8s that they hadn't used before and eight nicely built guys came out of them with guns and all. I immediately grabbed Alisa by the hand and started running as fast as I could. I heard them running after us but I didn't turn back. We went into the burnt down shopping centre through a hole a mortar made and hid in some small room on the first floor which must have been some sort of storage or a toilet. My gun was in the car. Fuck. I used my one hand to cover Alisa's mouth so they didn't hear her breathe and the other one for my mouth. The guy with a gun was walking past us, using his cellphone to light the way. He left and we stayed there for at least another half hour, in sweat and silence, thinking he was waiting somewhere in the building. Then we cautiously came out, found Iggy and turned back.

We guessed those were Ćelo's men but how did they know where we were? How did they know which car we were in? Eureka! We were working for Ćelo the whole time!

* * *

123

That evening, when we got back to Sarajevo, another, even crazier thing happened. On a deserted street, near the football stadium, Iggy abruptly stopped the car to avoid hitting a large black raven who was calmly standing in the road and looking at us. It looked like some sort of an apparition, a clear omen of a sort. It came to the car and jumped on the open window on my side. We were speechless, observing it all in great wonder. I don't know why but I felt no fear. Then the raven jumped on my right shoulder. His long beak was right next to my eye. There was utter silence in the car. It was incredibly weird. Iggy slowly started driving and raven rode with us for about fifteen minutes and only when we parked by the café we were driving to, he got on the window again, turned towards us, looked at each of us individually, and flew off towards the moonlight. We did not speak for the rest of the night. He left a feather on my shoulder and I carried it in my wallet for years to come. Until I lost my wallet.

* * *

Ćelo killed someone that night and got six years imprisonment for it. When he got out, we saw each other in some bar. He looked at me for a while, he knew me from somewhere but he couldn't remember where from. Before he could remember, I left.

A few days later he committed suicide. That is what the official report said. Unofficially, it is said that he was killed like a dog on his doorstep. The whole of the political and religious elite attended his funeral.

* * *

After a while, I went to a village with Alisa, got clean and stayed clean for almost six months.

* * *

I loved Mirna still and I wanted to be with her. One day I told Alisa. She was sad but she understood.

* * *

Mirna was at some acting workshop in Medjugorje then and on the anniversary of the start of our dating, 5 February 2001, she came back and I went to tell her that I was clean and good and that I loved her.

We had waited for this moment a long time. I ran up the stairs, keys in my hand, so I could go in without a sound, jump over the squeaking parts of the parquet floor and kiss her and hold her at last.

Those were my thoughts. The way I wanted it to be. The reality was somewhat different.

* * *

The echoes of the wide entrance hall are a mixture of the sounds of screaming, cries and calling of Mirna's name. I run up the stairs, through the door wide open and I see Mirna's mother, deformed from the pain, standing in front of the bathroom door. I come near, Mirna is in the bath. And then everything starts to shake and buzz violently, my peripheral sight is narrowing, and I start to see everything like through a keyhole. I want to scream, but have no voice. In all that buzzing, through that keyhole I see her mother getting into my face, grabbing me by the shoulders and shaking me, telling me something through tears but I can't hear her. I am trying to understand but no, I can't. I try lifting Mirna out of the bath but I can't move her frozen and stiff body. I touch her face and kiss her. I can still feel it under my fingers and on my lips. I lose myself and draw back. It's all a blur.

For a while I don't understand what's happening. Men in white taking out a stretcher from the bathroom. A stiff body covered with a white sheet. I see policemen, they ask me something. I don't understand it. I can't hear them through the buzzing.

"Miksi!" I shout. "No. No... Not you! Miksi! What is happening?".

The men in white come up to me, one is holding my hands and the other sticks a needle in me.

"Mirna is dead!"
Blackout.

* * *

I woke up in our bed. Alone. I wanted it all to be just a dream. But it wasn't. The pain tore me apart. A dark emptiness the size of universe spread through my chest. This enormous love, which had nowhere to go anymore was ripping my soul into atoms. I wanted to close my eyes and not open them ever again. It was unbearable. I got up and walked through the flat. There were a lot of people, yet it was silent. Only some quiet crying. I found a bottle of vodka and drank.

Blackout.

* * *

Four days later, I laid her into her grave.

* * *

Duško and I sat in the kitchen for months drinking. I moved in with him and slept in Mirna's room. I screamed from pain for months.

Then I started going out and causing problems in the city. Everyone avoided me. I was totally devastated. I wished for someone to kill me, as I didn't have the balls to do it myself. That's the worst. You can't kill yourself. You have to live with it. With brutal definity.

Mirna's mother turned to faith but since God doesn't exist, there was no help coming from above. There is no help. It was the end of life for all of us. I tried believing there was something up there and that she went to a better place but lying to myself didn't help. Denying death is immature.

I am not sure I can explain what happens in the brain when you lose someone you love so much but I do know that change is total and permanent. You can never return to what was before. I think that the brain gets electrocuted making all the synapses break, since all your plans for the future are linked to that one person and in your head, the future without her doesn't exist. Suddenly, there is this huge amount of data but it is no longer connected, as if someone just shook it out of the folder and into a pile and you don't know what to do with it. Total chaos. It is possible that it is a process that serves to re-connect the synapses differently, adjusting to new circumstances but from now on without the person you were connected to in thoughts and through pheromones. To reset and restart. But for us down here, we can't see those processes on a molecular level but just feel them as huge suffering and pain that is unbearable.

Duško suggested two options: one was to kill myself and the other was to stop thinking about her. He opted for the latter. That seemed horrible. How could he stop thinking of his own daughter? Was there a betrayal larger than that one?

* * *

After a while, I got asked to do a play in Bulgaria. I accepted, thinking I'd think about her less. It didn't work. I drank a lot; that was the only thing that made it better. We then took that play to Cairo to a festival there. I've been longing to visit Cairo my whole life and now, when I was there, I didn't feel like leaving the hotel. On the first day we saw the pyramids and a museum and that was all I saw. I sat in my room, drinking every day, all day. I didn't feel like living. I missed Mirna terribly. Heroin! Heroin was the only salvation. I don't know why I had waited that long. But it was the cure for everything and much less of a problem than the one I now had. I knew if I took that road there was no turning back because if I ever got clean I'd have to face reality. I wasn't ready for that and I believed I never would be. I would have to continue from this very spot I left off and I had no intention of returning here. I am not that brave. I believe I just opted for solution number one. I went down to the reception to find Ahmed, a guy who was trying to sell me two prostitutes wearing burkas and sat with him in the lobby. I didn't want to buy a cat in the bag and

I wasn't in that mood either. If anyone knew where to get Horse, it was him. OK, Ahmed said, I know a guy who knows some guys who could help you. We have to go to the other end of the town. The two of us and the two hookers drove for two and a half hours in a taxi with no air-conditioning under the African sun, through parts of town rarely visited by tourists. There was rubbish everywhere and a terrible stench. Houses built one on top of the other. The biggest cockroaches I ever saw covered the streets and it was hard to walk without crushing a few with every step you took. The streets were totally deserted, no one there except twenty or so boys walking behind me, laughing and shouting things at me because, as my guide said, they never saw a white man in real life before. The three of us waited for Ahmed in a 'restaurant' that looked and smelled more like a toilet than a restaurant. When he turned up with the heroin we got in the taxi and went back. The drive back was even longer because for reasons still unknown to us, people started coming out on the hot asphalt shouting 'Allahu Akbar'. Some great celebration kicked off but neither the taxi driver nor Ahmed knew what it was for. We somehow made it to the hotel. All I wanted was to get to my room so I could get high, but Ahmed and the hookers followed. Fuck them. We all came to my room. They took off their burkas. They were incredibly beautiful.

"Are you sure you don't want one? Or two?" my new friend asked.

"I am sure brother! I have better things to do. You just enjoy yourselves!" I replied, rolling a $20 bill.

The three of them went into the bathroom laughing and I sat on the big double bed in my spacious room of the Cairo Sheraton Hotel, unwrapped the packet and put the TV on louder so not to hear the sounds from the bathroom and snorted in a significant amount of the powder from the packet. My eyes stopped on the screen. A familiar, disgusting face. My trainer Abaz, or his even more evil twin! Under his photo it said Mohammad Ata. It was 11 September 2001.

Our stay in Cairo was extended due to all the flights being cancelled, so we spent another month at the Sheraton at the expense of the festival.

* * *

After that, I returned to Sarajevo back on Horse, worse than ever. I hit the bottom. I stole 3000 Marks from my grandfather who was like a father to me, money he saved for his funeral. I paid it back later, when he really needed it. My veins had retracted a long time ago. I was now injecting myself in the neck, in the thick vein on the forehead, in my palms, my soles and my penis that was black, yellow, green, blue and swollen in places. It looked like a colourful piece of ginger. When heroin passes through testicles the pain is paralyzing. On the soles and palms the skin is thick and it is hard to penetrate and if you use more force than necessary the needle can hit a bone. I hit up on the bus, in the tram, in a bar at a table, on the street, in parks. Twenty or thirty times a day, at half an hour intervals. I needed around 250 Euros each day. How did I get to that sort of money? Don't even ask but I did.

I caught myself running through the city if I was in a crisis, to con someone. Soaked in cold sweat, getting in a taxi and driving past the bar called Kogo that I always despised because of the normal people sitting there normally and drinking their coffee, looking at their girlfriends, going home, fucking or whatever they do, going out for a coffee again tomorrow and over and again. I used to tell myself they were stupid and boring and that my life was much better and more interesting but that they hadn't come to that stage of consciousness to recognise it and never will. How I hated them, out of pure envy as I wouldn't survive long enough to live it.

I knew all the junkies in the city and none of them was as bad as I was. I could shoot up three times the amount that anyone else did and still remain on my feet, whereas they'd die or end up in a hospital. The sorrow was breaking my family into pieces. I often saw my mother sitting in the dark and looking at the newspaper cut-outs she'd been collecting for years, and photo albums with my childhood photos. It must be terrible looking at your child disappear in front of your eyes and you not being able to do anything to save him.

* * *

My sister was in labour and she asked me to take her to the maternity hospital, since there was no-one else to do it. I was in withdrawal and didn't feel like it but all the dealers were sleeping anyway and there was nowhere to find drugs at two in the morning, so I went with her to the hospital and continued the withdrawal in the hospital corridor. Around four in the morning, she gave birth to a daughter, Romana. The midwife came out and thinking I was the father she gave her to me. I looked at this little creature, confused and ashamed to be in such miserable state, with dirty junkie hands, coloured with all the stabs and purulent holes, holding in my arms such purity and thinking how in few years, her parents will have to explain who her uncle is in the photos, the one who died young, probably omitting to say what of. It seemed that child was looking at me and recognising me. Suddenly, I didn't want to die anymore. Another process on a molecular level seems to have taken place. I swear that child saved my life, right there and then. I was on the same crossroads I was on in Cairo. The path I had chosen that had brought me here was behind me and ahead was one very new and uncertain. Behind my back was death and in front; life. I had to move on, regardless of everything. I knew what awaited and what I would have to face. I now understood Duško.

* * *

My friend Pjer was directing his first feature film. Although he knew I was using, he gave me a chance I couldn't miss. All of the earnings went on heroin. Dealers used to bring it every day to the film set for me. I took small doses, just so I could function.

* * *

After the filming and with my agreement, my mother locked me in the flat and took the key. I decided to shoot up one more time, the last time. I stole 20 Marks from her, called a dealer to bring me a packet to the back of the building, then stole some thread from Granny, tied it to a camera lens case, put the money in it and slid it down from the ninth floor. The dealer took the money, put the drugs into the case and I shot up for the last time in my life.

My folks figured out I was high, so they locked me up in my room and took the key. They didn't have to do that, as the decision had been made already.

Thoughts started arriving. I remembered the first time I took heroin. It was wonderful. I always dreamed of that feeling but it never came back. The warmth. The condition without a single desire. Heroin was the answer to all my questions, including the ones I never asked. A solution to all problems, cure to all fears, insecurities and sufferings. A secret that I didn't want to share with anyone. In Utero. Like a foetus in a placenta. Free, yet protected. I felt a new life growing inside of me. A baby. A sweet and hungry baby, who likes only one kind of food. As it grows, it becomes hungrier. I let it eat as much as it wanted and it grew quickly. It took over all the organs of my body and in the end, my brain as well. It started thinking and living independently. I became a tenant in my own body, without a right of say, and the rent increased all the time. The sweet baby became a beast with enormous appetites. Now I have to fight to regain my own body back. Organ by organ, cell by cell, synapse by synapse. And here I am, in an icy sweat, shackled by freedom. The epic struggle begins. The milky acid in the muscles started to spasm my body in terrible pain. The spasms threw me around the room uncontrollably and the strongest ones put me up on my feet, then I'd crash again. Days went on in the same fashion. Every prick I ever did with the needle started stinging like a bee sting. I had been on four or five grams a day and withdrawal was horrible, like nothing before it. And all I wanted to was to fly. And look at me know. Could one be further from it than this?

Suddenly, the room turns into a beautiful sunny meadow. Mirna and I are lying on the grass, bathed in sunlight, holding hands. We are looking at each other in endless love. Suddenly her hands become cold and stiff and her face starts disintegrating and rots to the bone, right in front of me. She sinks into the ground and is pulling me down with her. It was all very real. I screamed and hit my head against the wall hoping I'd lose consciousness and stop hallucinating. The room was all bloody. I didn't want to take any pills to ease the suffering, it could only be done like this or not at all. After several days of hell, the beast started retracting and shrinking. When it got to the size of a cockroach, I crushed it. That old cockroach was cornered so many times before but somehow it managed to survive, turned on his back with little feet tickling me all over my body. Now it was crushed. I opened the window, let the sun in and breathed in the air, filling my lungs. I think I still have particles of air from that day in my alveoli. It was crystal clear that heroin would never happen again.

* * *

Since then, I don't mention Mirna to anyone. When I catch myself thinking of her, I quickly turn my thoughts to something else. I practiced not thinking of her. Not a day passed without a thought but I learned to make them short. The pain didn't go away, I just got used to it.

* * *

On 28 December 2002, Mirna's birthday, Duško died.

* * *

My grandfather Milan was a deacon in the Orthodox church when he was young. Women had the hots for that, he used to say. In Second World War, he witnessed the Ustashe[15] raping and liquidating his nine-member family. He later repaid that debt in his own way.

Although a Serb by birthplace and an atheist by confession, he was a strategic consultant to the BiH Army during the war in the 1990s. During the Second World War, he had been a decorated Partisan in Tito's army. After the war he continued as a professional officer in the JNA although he had

---

15 Croatian fascists in WWII supported by catholic church.

publicly criticised the army and that's why he was on their blacklist to be 'taken out'. I think this big mouth of mine is from his gene pool. The day before the start of the war, our flat was showered by sniper bullets from our own police. A bullet went through my grandma's pot while she was holding it in her hands. Although that attack seemed like a mistake at the time, it wasn't. Scaring and sometimes killing of the non-Muslims was a part of the passive ethnic cleansing of the territory but I only figured that out a bit later. Milan was hurting because his JNA was killing civilians in Croatia, Slovenia and BiH. He couldn't come to terms with that. He was usually a cheerful old man but he got depressed at the start of the war and got better only at rare intervals. He went to see a shrink and was given Thorazine. Because I had lots of experience with drugs and psychiatry, I suggested he stop taking that therapy. He was told the same by my grandmother Dušanka, a retired psychologist.

One night when I went to have a shower after sex, as I came out of my room, I found him hanging on the gas pipe in the corridor. Two years to the day since Mirna died. On the same date. No goodbye letter. His right leg was still on the step of the folding ladder. Although I knew not to touch anything before the police arrived, I took a knife, cut the rope, laid him on the floor and then called the police.

I went to my room and told my accidental vis-
itor not to panic, that my grandpa had just committed suicide and that she had to jump over him
if she wanted to go home. She started screaming
and woke up my mother in the other room. While
I waited for the police that came eight and a half
hours later, I took off his wristwatch and 20 Marks
from his pocket. That night I sat with my mates in
a bar and ordered a round on my grandpa's tab. A
few days later we buried him. I was cool at the funeral, life experiences taught me to be well trained
to control my thoughts and emotions but the trum-
peter played some sad tune and tore me to pieces and got me into the heavy thoughts. Grandpa
was my role model. I killed him off with my drug
abuse, the JNA with their killing of civilians, worshippers of faith with their destruction and division of Yugoslavia. The primitives will destroy the
planet in the end. George Bush was getting ready
to invade Iraq and that could lead to a nuclear war.
Bush will go unpunished regardless as democracy
gives immunity to those most responsible for the
shit on this planet. Democracy needed serious up-
grading.

I felt I had to do something regarding the attack
on Iraq.

* * *

It took me some seven days to organise the first protests against the war in Iraq. Only a few thousand gathered but for BiH that was democratic progress unseen until then as those were the first demonstrations in the country after the war. A little after that, workers started coming out on the streets, demanding their rights.

The next time, my friend Wesley, an American architect, was my right hand in the organisation. But he got a call from the US Embassy and retracted his part in it. The same day that he went back to New York, he was hit by a car. The doctors barely patched Wesley up and the perpetrators were never found.

When we got in front of the US Embassy, we were joined by a group of extremists who were shouting 'Allahu Akbar'. They outnumbered us significantly and they simply took over. I publicly denounced them and left the protest. I am a pacifist. Destruction can't fix anything. That's why I got a number of threats those days not just from them, but from nationalists of all three faiths. These threats gave me an idea to make a porn film about all of them, where all three, each wearing their own uniforms, would make love until exhaustion.

The news of the porn film ended up on almost all front pages, news portals, radio and TV stations. And then one day I heard loud banging on my door. I looked through the peephole and saw a Wahabi there. My grandpa had a gun hidden somewhere, a war trophy from the Second World War but only God knew where he hid it. I looked again through the peephole and through piles of hair, I recognised the face of my good old Krepo.

"Come in my brother! I hope you will not explode on me?" I said laughing.

Krepo turned to Islam and the teachings of Muhammad ibn Wahhab but he did not turn to the hatred that usually accompanies this doctrine in vast amounts. We talked about everything, as always but the main topic was the religious porn film and you could see he had sincere concerns for my life. Krepo had got married, got a daughter and with help of religion, stopped using heroin. We were always extreme about everything, so his choice did not surprise me.

"Do you ever think of heroin?" I asked.

"Every day!" my honest friend replied and sighed while scratching his belly.

As always, I enjoyed our chat. Krepo hasn't changed, he just got a little hairier. He runs a centre for non-violent action, organising meetings of war veterans from previously opposing sides, trying to reconcile them but reconciliation is in no one's interest here. Hatred is where fortune lies.

I told him about an event the previous winter. Unimportant on the surface but it was a very educational sociological experiment in my opinion.

I was on the Olympic mountain near Sarajevo, at some Red Bull event in which competitors attempt to take off into the air in handmade, human-powered flying machines by racing them down a frozen track and inevitably falling into the water pool at the end. It's a joyful marketing trick at low cost, you know what I'm talking about. The audience was divided in two with the ice track in the centre for the competitors. At one point a heavy, wet snowball flew from the right side to the left. Then someone from the left side threw a snowball to the right. Right then a horrible fratricidal snowball conflict commenced.

Many ended up in ER. I got one in my face and thought I'd lost my eyes. How did a snowball result in such destructive energy? Then I realised it was not a snowball but a piece of the ice track. The semantic line someone had randomly drawn between the two sides, made for two enemy factions among worshipers of the same faith and hatred appeared between them for no real reason and without announcement. The powerful, blinding emotion, with no option to comprehend the weight of the situation and its possible consequences, lifted their euphoria, initiated action and awoke a primitive instinct. Although everyone on the left must have known only one person was responsible for the first snowball, they did not think twice about punishing the whole group (including children sitting on their parents' shoulders) and randomly hurling missiles towards them, purely because they were on the other side of a line. They held the whole group responsible, without exception. Grown-ups and children. I am telling you, it was not the reaction of intelligent beings and yet they could not resist it. It was a compound of utterly wrong chemicals in the brain, the heritage of Homo Erectus, Sahelanthropus Tchadensis or an even further ancestor, that might have been needed at that time. Our version of the ancient bad drugs they were hooked on. When you draw the line, they get high. It's their drug.

* * *

Those days, as part of anti-war protest, I erected a number of artistic installations around the city with a 'Make Love Not War' slogan. For the most famous one, where I put three condoms on the three fingers of the statue of Jesus Christ at the Sarajevo Cathedral, and a 'Peace' sign around his neck, I nearly ended up in prison. The whole world wrote about that particular installation, even the Pope John Paul spoke on Radio Vatican to say how Catholicism was in danger.

The Church accused me of desecration of a sacred building and pronounced me a criminal. The punishment prescribed by law was one year. I don't think there was a single trial in the short history of this country that has attracted so much media attention. Not even the trials of war criminals. A very small group of people worked out the symbolism of my installation and the religions, as expected, used it for what they usually do; to spread hatred and raise tensions. This one was like it was served on a platter for them. Still, the installation managed to achieve the unthinkable by uniting all three confessions. Uniting them in hatred towards me but still it united them.

I looked at the law in detail and realised that they couldn't lock me up based on these charges because it stated that desecration is a 'change of shape or damage or ruin to the sacred object', which was not the case in this instance. I suggested to them that they should sue me for slander on religious grounds because I would then maybe get six months imprisonment if they could prove that was my intention. They didn't take my advice.

* * *

After the acquittal, a funny thing happened. An elderly gentleman called me on the phone, he said his name was Mario Kopić and asked me if I would meet him, as he was doing some charity work for blind children.

"Of course," I said, "I'd love to help and volunteer."

I had an idea anyway to do a play for the blind that would be based on sounds and smells. So, we met. Mario was a feminine old man with thinning grey hair and a white goatee. We started talking and our conversation went on for more than an hour, but blind children didn't get to be a topic. I was being well-mannered and didn't interrupt. He was talking about his mother whom he loved dearly, their endless love towards each other and Jesus Christ.

"I see you have no respect for religion!" he said and I replied:

"Dear sir, religion is an international criminal organisation, responsible for the deaths of hundreds of millions of people, money laundering, tax evasion and lots more. You know what I am talking about! The organisation is run by a few greedy psychopaths who falsely present themselves as 'messengers of God' and 'experts on the secret of eternal life', and purposely, with the aim of getting themselves rich, they use methods of fear and in doing so, do not shy away from initiating even the bloodiest of conflicts to reach their aim. We, the people who all have the same ancestors, and this is genetically proven, so are all blood related, have been in a two thousand year long fratricidal war for the sake of the profit of that organisation. In a world where we call upon justice, this organisation has been pronounced legal and not only have the perpetrators not been brought to

justice for bringing us to the verge of extinction but we are also paying for it.

The genocide at Srebrenica was preceded by a holy mass, during which an Orthodox priest blessed the 'Scorpios' special unit, so that they could commit terrible atrocities in the name of God.

That Orthodox priest was never brought before the courts, nor he will be, although he was inciting crimes and I don't like the concept that anyone is above the law. By some logic, the punishment for incitement should be identical to the punishment for command responsibility. The Church never distanced itself from it. On the contrary, they hid the criminals and canonised them.

Or the priest that blessed the tanks that flattened villages with civilians inside? Later, when he was caught and recorded fornicating with four juveniles, he simply pretended he had lost the ability to speak. He didn't spend a day in prison.

You want me to respect that? What is wrong with you, for God's sake? Are you sane?

Or the Catholic concentration camps in Herzegovina? I can't remember if the Pope distanced himself from all those atrocities that his followers did with a cross in their hands, in the name of Christ and Catholicism but he did speak to attack the peace installation I put up. The Catholic Church in this country greeted every single war criminal with a holy mass upon their return from prison after they *served their sentence. Holy mass for the greatest filth there is?*

To those that killed civilians, including children? Am I to respect them? Or maybe Caco, who as well as forty civilians, also massacred nine young policemen and after that the Islamic community buried him like a hero. Should I respect that? No way. I see only believers celebrating these monsters, I am sorry but no, I don't respect that. Respect has to be earned.

The most horrible thing in all of that is that those people haven't an ounce of guilt on their conscience, no sympathy towards the victims, no emotions. They think killing and raping people of other religions (or those without a religion) is an act of goodness and they call themselves good people! I spent time with that kind in the nut house! Do they know what rape does to a woman? Do they know what the killing of a child does to a family? Of course they do, that's why they do it! They are not and cannot be heroes that the religions present them to be. I am appalled by the amount of hatred with which religion has contaminated humanity. I don't respect their followers because I now know what all they are capable of and who their idols are. I don't respect their shrines, traditions or customs. I don't respect anything that causes violence and division among people. You have to understand me, I am a witness to religious madness, that should be cataloged under exactly that name in psychiatric textbooks.

Sometimes I think, what would happen if aliens came?

Alien 1: We've been observing you from above for a while now and I have to confess that some things are not quite clear to us. For example, we see a number of you carrying metal objects firing things. Is that how you produce energy?

Me: Oh no, those are rifles and they serve to kill people who don't believe in the same things that these others do.

Alien 1: Killing? I don't understand. Tell me, we see some small explosions, is that how you produce energy?

Me: No, those are bombs, also for killing, we have larger ones as well, to kill a larger number of people.

Alien 1: Oh, so. What do you mean by killing, like taking a life from another living being? And what do you do with them then? Bring them back to life?

Me: No. We bury them.

Alien 1: Hmm, Interesting. Is it some sort of a game? Does that mean you resolved the question of immortality?

Me: Well, yes, in theory. Those people believe that when they die they will come back to life and that is why they kill each other but in practice...

Alien 1: So you kill them, bury them and that is it? But, why?

Me: I don't kill them. You see the one kind walking around the large stone cube, they hate the ones who hit their head against the wall because they think that some supreme, horrible but yet compassionate being loves those walking around the cube more than those hitting their head against the wall and vice versa. Then there are the third ones, who wear a miniature dead man nailed to a torture device around their neck, then the fourth...

Alien 1: *Urgh! That's quite morbid!*

Me: *Trust me, it's nothing. Fourth, then fifth, there are 4200 different kinds, and they are all totally convinced they are the ones who are right.*

Alien 1: *Ha-ha-ha, I am dying with laughter!*

Me: *No, really. I am serious. In principle, those who kill the most believe that a long unintelligent animal, without speaking apparatus, talked a woman (made by this creature from a rib of a man it created out of clay), into eating an apple which...*

Alien 2: *Are you fucking with us?*

Me: *I am not, I swear!*

Alien 2: *Let's get out of here!*

Me: *Stop, let's have a drink!*

Alien 2: *Oh fuck off, will you!*

Me: *But we are not all like that, there are some of us who are sane. Wait, don't go! Don't leave me here! Nooooo....*

I'd die of shame if I bumped into them.

It is not clear to me why someone decides not to know the truth about everything? Not to want to know that the wind doesn't blow out of some hole God controls but that it is created by vertical movement of air due to the ground heating, that tsunamis and earthquakes happen due to tectonic movements and not God's will. Why don't they want to know that and it is all so incredibly interesting. Why have they decided to live in the dark? Why do they spend their whole short life thinking about death? Death is ever so ordinary, there is as much spirituality in it as there is in a TV when you unplug it from the wall. How come they don't find the story of God creating light on the first day and the Sun only on the third strange? I can't even pretend to respect the fact that someone can't understand the world around them."

"God can make people see and get up from their wheelchairs!" said Mario in response.

"Really? I admit, I've heard of that but have never seen it, I've only seen people often losing their eyes or ending up in the wheelchair."

"All as deserved!"

"Are you saying that my friends, who gave their arms, legs, eyes and life for this shit called this country, deserved it? You know what? They probably have. Are you telling me right now that children because of whom we have met here today, deserved to be blind and that believers sitting in the first rows in houses of worship, our politicians and religious clerks responsible for all this corruption, crime and poverty, they haven't?"

"I wanted to say that God truly exists and he decides!"

"Truly? The truth us a very subjective thing. Your truth that God exists is totally opposite to mine; that it doesn't. Both are true, it just depends on the point of view."

"You've hurt the feelings of a worshipper!"

"I have as much concern for the feelings of worshippers as they do for mine. Worshippers can't tell good from evil. Good is theirs and evil is someone else's. That did not prove to be a relevant method to determine guilt before the Hague tribunal."

"You have desecrated our saviour!"

"I've put up an art installation on a statue, a figure made out of plaster, a totem, an idol. On it, I found a thick layer of dust and bird shit which should have been cleaned off by someone who worshipped it but they didn't. With that installation I tried to say the same thing as the 'saviour' did before the Romans nailed him on the torture device and then took the copyrights for his persona and acts."

"That is not a torture device, it is a cross and a symbol of the saviour's suffering."

"Sir, if the Romans had by any chance executed Jesus in some other manner and not the crucifixion but say, hanging for example, the Christians today wouldn't be called 'Christians' but rather 'Noosists' and in honour of the noose that they would then wear one around their necks or perhaps wear the *hung body of Jesus Christ hanging on their necks. Try imagining all the Christians wearing that kind of pendant instead of the cross around their necks. Does that look morbid or distasteful, not to say horrible? If that was so and if that symbol of the hanged Jesus was widely accepted as normal, if I would appear then in public with a miniature symbol of a corpse nailed to the torture device... pardon me... to the cross, people would then declare me morbid and sick. And now try to look at the wider picture. Try to understand what it means for humankind now when children from birth are getting used to seeing a mutilated human body nailed to a cross. To put it simply, that horrifying, utterly morbid and sick image becomes totally normal and not morbid or sick as it is and should be, as it graphically depicts what people are capable of doing to one another in their twistedness. And children, who grow up looking at this every day, everywhere they go, they don't see it as sick and twisted but normal instead. Why are we then surprised by the horrible things people do to one another these days? A corporation whose logo is something so twisted, morbid and sick is exactly that: twisted, morbid and sick. Don't lose your nerve, everything I say is just my opinion, nothing more. I hope you don't think that for some reason you have more right to freedom of thought and speech because you don't. And no matter how hard you believe in something, faith doesn't make things real, you just*

believe it does. While faith, like lack of faith is noth-
ing else but a feeling like any other: love, hate, fear,
guilt. It's nothing else but a combination of chemical
compounds on receptors in your brain and not ex-
isting anywhere outside of it. I hope you know that?
Those are now quite old scientific facts. Your love ex-
ists nowhere else but your head, isn't that so? Be it
the love for your mother or God. How would then
your hate be anywhere else but there? Why would
your faith be somewhere else? Or God?"

"I have to go to mass."

"Great, ask him for peace in the world. But ask
nicely, make sure you concentrate and focus, not
sloppily, like you've done so far."

I didn't want to dissuade him. It is a great priv-
ilege to be a minority in this country. The truth is
not for everyone. I didn't want to get into a discussion with him. I just wanted to help blind children,
but they were not even mentioned.

I thought he probably wouldn't contact me
again but few days later he did call and we met
again. He asked me if I would like to go and study
or live somewhere, anywhere else in fact. He said
he'd pay for my flat, tuition and expenses. I wasn't
taking him up on it.

"Thank you," I said, "There's no need, I'm fine
here!

Again, not a mention of blind children, which
was all rather strange.

"Come tonight for the premiere of the film, 'Jesus F. Christ'!" I said. It was a short film we had made showing me putting the installation on the statue.

The premiere went well, I made a short speech and invited everyone for a drink at the end. Just then, Mario came out of nowhere, gave me an envelope and then left without saying a word. It was a letter glorifying Jesus and saying how I shouldn't have set up that installation, blah, blah, blah. A film critic who writes his review before the premiere! After that, I didn't see or hear from Mario for almost a year, until one day I agreed to meet a girl in front of the Sarajevo Cathedral at 5.45pm.

Four bodyguards, with one Catholic priest in the middle, walked past me, some two metres away and entered the Cathedral. The priest looked familiar, so I thought to myself that I must have seen him on TV. Two or three hours must have passed before it dawned onto me; Mario Kopić! He was the priest I just saw. The name was fake, of course. I tried finding him on the internet with no success but later I saw him number of times on the TV. He always sat on the Cardinal's right-hand side.

* * *

One day, a few people landed in paraglider near the set of a film I was working on. Well, that is it! I have to become a pilot, I totally forgot about that. I walked up to them, introduced myself and asked if I could buy the kit somewhere. They dialled a few numbers and I bought my first aircraft.

I taped up a metre-wide tear on the old wing and took off. It was quickly clear that whoever said that bit about, "Heroin feels like flying" had never flown in their lives! That saying had fucked me up quite significantly in life. Heroin was a really bad substitute for this. Flying was much better than all my expectations and they were pretty high to begin with.

* * *

I talked my friend Nerko into flying in a very strong wind. He injured his spine but recovered in five or six months as he hadn't damaged his spinal cord. I had the same injury later. Three times.

* * *

The first twenty or so flights, I ended up in trees. But I didn't give up. When the glue started giving in, the craft would suddenly begin diving and I'd find myself on top of a tree in some forest but my desire to fly was much stronger than the fear of it.

* * *

Once I walked into Romana's room by accident and saw her holding a metal hair pin in the socket, whilst trying to put another in the other hole. "NO!", I screamed loudly. She got scared and started crying, sadly and loudly. We are even now, I thought.

* * *

Since I was unemployed, I falsified some paperwork to get a loan from the bank. I bought a Honda.

* * *

The day I got my license, I talked my friend Jasa into riding around town with me. He fell off the bike and hit his head on a stone flowerpot by the road. He was in a coma for two months and has never fully recovered. I fell off as well but with no such consequences.

* * *

I carried adrenaline across the border, my new drug that was impossible to discover, even by sniffer dogs.

* * *

Winters here are quite cold, long and boring, so with lack of anything to do, I became a serious alcoholic. I ended up in the abdominal surgery department, where, as a terminal patient, I was waiting for my death. What else? I was connected to machines, with some pipe sticking out of my nose and through it, into a bag on the floor, litres and litres of thick black liquid poured from the bottom of my stomach. On my right I heard the quiet but unbearable sound of the even beeping of my heart on the ECG. I was trying to breathe air in as slowly as possible to avoid the pain in my unnaturally swollen abdomen, a pain similar to someone emptying a magazine in it. Maybe someone did, I can't remember.

It was actually swollen due to the inflammation of my pancreas, lungs, kidneys, liver and heart. Can the heart even be inflamed? I was staring at the neon light above me and contemplating the passing of life. How did I get here? It was my birthday yesterday; I remember drinking maybe two or three litres of red wine and then moving onto Vodka-Red Bulls. And that is where the scene ended. How was it possible that I got myself into this state? Had I learned nothing? I had replaced heroin with another, no less dangerous, but socially more acceptable heavy drug. Five years of my life almost disappeared from my memories and those that haven't, I'd rather they had.

I remember how one morning the police beat me nearly to death at their station because the night before I was caught near the Cathedral with seven frozen chickens stolen from a nearby grill that I had broken into, and after the arrest I managed to escape handcuffed from their car. I remember the trial and the jury that couldn't believe what kind of unique idiot was standing in front of them. I remember the acquittal, albeit a probationary one and the laughter that my serious confession caused in the courtroom as I stated that Jack Daniels himself committed this crime while I, as merely a witness can confirm all the points in the charge presented by the prosecution. This was not far from the truth. I stole frozen chickens? WTF, I never did anything that idiotic even when I was on heroin. Alcohol was pure evil.

I remember women, but not their faces. Naked bodies in toilets of stinky bars, hallways, lifts, dark alleyways and piss filled passages.

If I ever write about life, this period deserves a book on its own, I thought to myself.

What will I do if I survive? I know! I'll set up a small airline for panoramic flights above the city.

Obviously, I survived and as soon as I got out I bought a motor-glider for two and for the first time, fully sober, experienced the whole pleasure of flying. My life started the day I stopped drinking. Pancreatitis saved my life.

* * *

At a pilot's summit, I met people from the parachute school centre in Banja Luka and that's how
that started. My friend Mirvad and myself went to
do our first jump. As soon as we landed, we took
the next parachute and jumped again, to get rid of
the fear.

* * *

As my friend Refik would say, "There isn't a situation in life where it is as clear as it is when at 4000m
you separate from the plane, that: if the parachute
is folded badly, there is no force that can save you."

* * *

I talked Refik into jumping the first time, as well as
the rest of the crew: Kuđa, Aldin, Ćazim, Elvir, Adi,
Marija, Nedim, Sany, Darko, Koja, Igor, Boris...
Amra. After the first jump, they didn't need any
more convincing. We were there every weekend.
We slept in the dorms at the airport. Sometimes
we'd take large telescopes from the astronomy club,
set them up at night in the middle of the track and
look at the galaxies and stars and their distances
and chemical composition. Early in the morning,
we'd wake up, fold the parachutes, fuel the plane

and jump all day long. Soul resting. A total distance from the disgusting everyday life of BiH. It was the nicest period in my life up to then. Parachutists from all over ex-Yugoslavia would come and we used to hang out like in the good old days.

That is where I met a lot of members of the 63rd Parachute Brigade, the same ones I fought against some fifteen years ago. Now we packed each other's parachutes and jumped together.

* * *

Amra jumped until we found out she was jumping with a baby in her belly. Our daughter Aya.

* * *

In the wintertime I didn't drink but acted in movies and the fees were sufficient to cover the cost of my adrenaline needs. The airline company didn't quite start the way I planned, as there was no school in the country for a craft of that type, so self-taught I managed to have many breakdowns which forced me to constantly order new parts that I'd have to wait sometimes a whole month or longer for. And sometimes a whole season would pass in waiting.

* * *

Four of us paragliding pilots set off to a world competition in acrobatic flying in Nepal. There should have been five of us, but Mirvad injured his spine in his paraglider. His left leg was paralysed after the accident but with the use of new and untested medicine, he managed to get the nerves in the spinal cord connected and with hard training he almost fully recovered. Needless to say that I talked him into flying that day!

* * *

We went to Nepal a year after their ten year-long civil war which had resulted in 12,000 people being killed. 12,000 people in ten years? What peace-loving people! The Orthodox used to kill that many in a few days back home.

* * *

He flew into a sunset, high above the red clouds, past the frozen Himalayas which rose above the clouds by another six kilometres. Eagles flew beside him; he could touch their wings.

* * *

One night, on a mountain near Sarajevo, whilst we were lying on a blanket watching the Perseids meteor shower in the sky, Amra went into labor. We said goodbye to the crew and set off to the maternity hospital. On that day, with clean hands and no shame, I held our daughter Aya in my arms.

* * *

In a local newspaper that my mother collected, I found an old interview that I'd given. They asked me who I'd like to work with most when it comes to big movie names. My reply was, "Brad Pitt and Angelina Jolie".

* * *

I went to a movie casting in Sarajevo. A few days later, I got a phone call from Gail, a famous casting director, who told me that it was actually Angelina Jolie directing the film, it was entitled 'In the Land of Blood and Honey' and that she wanted to see me for the role of Peter.

* * *

The only emotion that overcomes me on the mention of the name of my country for a long time now is huge shame. Angelina was coming as the UN Goodwill Ambassador, to make a war film about raped women to get the attention of the international community and to start and speed up court proceedings against the rapists.

Sensationalist right-wing media, starving for clickbait, started spreading fake news that the script had a Muslim woman fall in love with her rapist. This disinformation started a lynch mob with the chair of the association of raped women, and very close to the ruling party, being the loudest. It all looked and smelled badly of extortion. Angelina figured it out quickly and moved the whole set to Hungary.

This was one of the biggest embarrassments ever. I think the whole world after this thought, "Why the hell did we save them?"

I simply couldn't keep my mouth shut. I wrote an open letter to the main Sarajevo news portal saying how ashamed I was to be a Bosnian because of this... and so, to my great surprise, I became public enemy number one!

But there was a couple thousand people who were also ashamed, who liked my words and who after all these two decades of religious tyranny, wanted to shout from the top of their lungs the same words that I had dared to say.

* * *

Me and my small family went to Hungary.

The filming started and Angie and I talked more and more about life. We had a lot in common. She rode an Augusta and I rode a Honda. She flew planes and I flew paragliders. We both parachuted. We chatted about stormy pasts, drugs and alcohol... Then Brad came. A simple, down-to-earth guy, a pilot and a biker too, and I can say that we got to be friends unusually quickly.

* * *

A few months after the filming ended, Angie and Brad invited us to be their guests in Hollywood. In the penthouse of the Roosevelt Hotel, where we were staying, they threw us a party.

So, that's what I was doing here, at this hotel.

"Angie tells me you had a hell of a life," Brad said.

"I'm not sure what to say."

"Sit down and write!"

"Write what?"

"Throw it all on paper and we'll make a film! It's interesting!"

"Maybe. Where should I start?"

"Here. Start from the top of this hotel and how you came to be here."

"How come I am in this job or in this hotel?"

"Whichever. Just write!"

The waitress came with a tray. He took the Jack with two ice cubes. I just had water due to my fucked up liver and pancreas.

"OK, bro. I'll email you."

* * *

After Hollywood, I returned home, wrote some eighty pages, attached them to an email and sent to Angelina and Brad. Then returned to Sarajevo reality: good old religious frenzy, hatred, intolerance, corruption, crime, etc... standard. My Aya was a few months old, a beautiful shiny dot in the medieval dark age that voters had chosen ever so democratically.

* * *

I suspected for a long time I had hepatitis C, and a blood test proved it. Treatment was required rather urgently and the medication, Interferon, was free for those with health insurance but for those of us who were jobless it cost a fortune. It's hard to make any plans for the future when you have hepatitis C, especially if it is A1, the African genotype which is hardest to cure. I needed a future because of Aya. So, I had to get a job to get the health insurance, and to get a job I had to graduate, and to graduate, I had to pass exams. Fine. Let's begin.

* * *

Amila and Belma, two colleagues in their fourth year asked me to do the graduation performance together. I had now been a student for eighteen years in total. I hadn't let the studies get in the way of my drug habit.

* * *

Angelina texted me, "So real I can smell it!"

A few days later, Brad replied to my email, "Wow, I've never read anything as crazy as this in my life. See you in New York, we'll talk details then, can't wait!"

* * *

A month later and ten exams passed, I graduated. It wasn't terribly hard. It would be a while before I got a job, so a while to get treatment as well.

* * *

My Facebook profile started looking like a revolutionary radio station with tens of thousands of followers. It was an oasis of peace visited by well-intended people from all over ex-Yugoslavia. An oasis that was a thorn in a side of the nationalists as it begun to connect everything they'd been trying to break into pieces for the past two decades. Wonderful things were put into motion and since I'd got the momentum, I let them roll.

* * *

It was a divine December day when I landed at JFK. A limo took me to the Waldorf Astoria Hotel. At the entrance, a doorman with Ed written on his name badge opened the car door and said, "Fedja, welcome to New York, I am Edin from Bihać".

As he was helping me get my things up to my room, he revealed all the secrets of the hotel, such as where and when you can eat for free. I can't say I didn't use that insider's tip. In my room, I found a welcome note on the bed and timings for TV appearances. I had a quick shower, sat on the Art Deco bed and dialed reception. After giving her Refik's number, the receptionist played Sinatra's 'New York, New York' while I was on hold. Sinatra lived in this hotel, so did Nikola Tesla. The weather outside changed and the clouds became low and dark. While I was listening to Sinatra, it started raining. The music was interrupted by Refik who gave me an address that I wrote on a piece of paper.

Ed was standing outside, in front of the hotel. He whistled loudly and stopped me a taxi in the pouring rain. When I got in, the black driver asked me where I was from and I said, "Bosnia."

"Boston?" he said.

"Yeah, I wish," I thought to myself. Some cool jazz tune played, and the driver softly sang every solo. People were pushing along on the sidewalks and hitting each others' umbrellas, while the cars barely moved. Refik lived three blocks away but it took us an hour and a half to get to him. New York was decorated for Christmas and I couldn't get enough of it.

Refik's cousin was at his place, as well as his wife and kids. His cousin Emir had come from New Zealand few months back and was now an active participant in the Occupy Wall Street movement in New York. He heard about my activities and the installation and we agreed to do something next time he was in Bosnia. I presented an idea to Refik that we set up a production house to be called Relative Pictures, named after relative jumping (the figure where parachutists hold hands during freefall). After a great time together, I went back to my hotel room, hoping to sleep at least a few hours. But as I was jetlagged, I decided to go to the hotel gym at 4am and only after that did I manage to fall asleep.

The next day, I went to Anderson Cooper's show with Angelina. After the show, we met Brad at the Waldorf to talk about Blank. He suggested Forster to direct it. Both him and Angie were suggesting I play myself but I was suggesting Brad do it. I also suggested Pjer wrote the script. We left it there until we met again.

The next day was the premiere of Blood and Honey and afterwards we all went to the Boom

Boom Room and hung out. Emir was there and Refik as well with the family. The trip was creative and inspirational and then came the return to the religious madness.

* * *

Reis was the Grand Mufti, Head Imam, famous at home for his aggressive nationalist outbursts whilst presenting a totally opposite image of himself internationally; that of the peacemaker, a uniting factor, the initiator of inter-religious dialogue, etc. I had been receiving threats from his fan club, via Facebook and email, ever since the first demonstration against the war in Iraq.

With his aggressive imposing of Islam through the schools and media, the atmosphere he created in this part of the world contributed to the strong radicalisation of Muslims. The Helsinki Committee for Human Rights sent a protest letter to the Islamic community because of the statements of this religious leader directed against those of different opinions. Embassies pointed out his radical and aggressive statements against the LGBTQ population, atheists, NGOs and members of other religious communities. One of his opponents, a politician who tried to get religious studies taken out of the school curriculum, found a bullet in front of his door, as a mafia threat to stop his activities.

After this, the politician quit his ministerial position in fear of his life and the lives of his family.

Not knowing any of this, an Italian foundation nominated him for an international peace award.

I started an online petition to prevent the award. The threats I received through social media and internet portals went beyond the morbid messages that I was used to and threats to my family soon started. I had to report these sick calls to have my family tortured, raped and beheaded to the police.

* * *

Angelina's film was showing at the Berlin Film Festival. My connecting flight was delayed, and I arrived in Berlin a few hours late. I ran out of the car straight onto the red carpet where I was greeted with a huge hug from Angie and Brad. After the screening and awards, we went to an artwork auction. Brad and Angie were competing against one another as to who would pay more for some scribbles as all the money was going to charity. The premiere of her film was scheduled in Sarajevo in two days time and I wasn't sure if I should tell them that I was currently at war with the Islamic Community and that it was possible that there would be an incident. I said nothing, hoping the police and other local and foreign security services would be serious when it came to safety at the event. I was also hoping that people were not crazy enough to cause a problem in front of so many journalists and the 20,000 people coming to the Sarajevo premiere. But then, who knows?

After they saw the film, all those who did all in their power to prevent the film being make in Sarajevo were coming up to her, congratulating her, kissing her hand and praising her. Sickening images to see from where I was standing. After the whole of the religious and political leadership congratulated her for the film, I whispered in her ear, "You just shook hands with the best organised mafia in Europe!"

"I know, I've seen it turning that way everywhere," she said, with a wide smile on her face, so nobody could work out what we were talking about.

* * *

After all went well, I told them what I'd gotten myself into and they suggested that I move with my family to their flat in New York but out of decency, I couldn't accept that generous offer. Then I introduced them to Pjer and left them to talk about work on the script. After they left, it was back to reality.

* * *

At the time, I was living under a lot of different pressures. I found my stability in parachuting. After you dive from a plane, there are few things that can rattle or scare you.

I dived until our club aircraft went down. Two guys, Nikola and Srdjan, set off on their first dive and with them, Alen the pilot and Nemanja and Stefan, the instructors. All lost their lives in the burning wreck of a Cessna. Amra, Boris and I each tattooed the registration number of the plane on the inside of our upper arms. Boris later got killed on a motorbike in Portugal.

* * *

There was a vacancy in the Chamber Theatre 55. They were looking for an actor. I got a job.

* * *

And then an incredible thing happened. It started when a girl called Jelena asked people on Facebook to help a homeless man, Ramiz, and his dog.

I had a garage where I kept my bike and diving and flying kit, but we managed to move things around and put a mattress and a gas heater in there. So Ramiz and his dog started living there.

Some time later, a guy named Loris posted a photo of another homeless man Dževad, also with a dog. I called Loris and suggested that we rent a garage for him. I went to an ads page and posted that I was looking to rent a garage to house a homeless man and his dog and that I'd pay 120 Marks per month. A German woman replied and said she would rent a studio flat to the homeless man, for 100 a month. I had no idea what to do, as I was totally broke, but I had found a place for the guy.

Facebook status; "I found a place for a homeless man, 100 marks per month, will someone help?". Two minutes later, Mirvad wrote, "One month on me". Then Arnan, also a paraglider pilot wrote, "One from me as well". Dina, "Three from me". Suad, Krepo, Željko, Amela, Brane, Amra, Selma, Edin, Refik, Jasmina, Adela, Sanela, Zoka, Đuro, Duca, Aldin, Nedeljko, Ivica, Valentina... Bosnians and Herzegovinians from all over the world. My inbox was filling up, as well as the bank account I had posted. The day after, as happy as one can be, I went to see the homeless guy Dževad, to introduce myself and tell him some people, in a joint effort, had managed to find him a place fit for a human to live. In disbelief, he got into my car and I took him to see the place. Through tears, he told me his life story. His daughter and son turn their heads away from him when they see him begging on the streets. They don't give him any money, they are ashamed of him. A mortar took half of his leg and he could barely walk, he was also hit by a sniper in the hip. But luckily, the new place was one stop away from the place where did his begging and with the bus he could get dropped right in front of the flat. I took him back to his workplace and told him I'd be back there to pick him up at 11am the following day, as I had to fix the place up for him first.

The landlady sent me an email offering to give him dishes, a cupboard and a bed. All I had to do is come earlier tomorrow and take it up from one floor below. People on Facebook offered blankets, gas heaters and dog food.

I drove around town and loaded all these donations into my car. Before going to bed, I checked a few times that no one had broken into my car and stolen it all. I barely slept that night because of all the good thoughts running through my head. As I was up early the next day, I went to the studio to fix it up a bit but on the way I stop to see Dževad, to see how he was and if he was excited. I saw him cross the street past me and in passing, over his shoulder he said, "I'm not going to live there".

It is hard for me to tell you now how I felt there and then. I basically felt like a moron. As if someone had slapped me across the face and ran away. For about ten minutes, I stood in the middle of the road. Like a donkey. And the first thought that came to my head was, "Never mind, at least it is a good story, I should write it down". Then the second thought occurred, "I know exactly what you mean, bro." I put on a smile, shrugged my shoulders and went on my way.

In the evening, I got on my computer to ask the people who sent money what to do with it. And then I noticed a link for a TV show on my Facebook wall. I saw Sergej, a Serbian actor I played in a movie with, and I saw he had posted a call to help a girl called Tijana from Belgrade who urgently needed a heart transplant.

Immediately, I asked the people who sent money for Dževad, to transfer money to her account and they all agreed. I called Sergej but he didn't pick up. I was too excited. I post on his wall, "Sergej. We want to help Tijana. Greetings from Sarajevo."

As this was the first interaction of this kind between the 'sides at war', it became news headlines across the Balkans instantly. Yugoslavia was on its feet, all together again. No hatred, no fear. Everyone joined in. That day we raised $500,000.

In the meantime, money for the homeless guy that was to be transferred to Tijana was still coming into my account. I was waiting for all of it to go in and then I'd transfer it to Belgrade in one go to avoid paying money transfers a number of times, as I'd prefer Tijana to get the money rather than some fat banker to by new rims for his *Cayenne*. Sergej then told me that all the money needed for Tijana had already been collected. So I told him that I would transfer what I had to a guy in Sarajevo who needed a lung transplant. So the money intended for the homeless guy, then to Tijana, in the end was given to a third person. And everyone was happy: the homeless guy who, after a sleepless night, realised he preferred freedom to being closed up in a box; Tijana, for whom the money was successfully collected and who went to Houston for surgery; the guy who suddenly got the money for his lung transplant operation; a guy from 'west' Mostar, to whom the people of 'east' Mostar transferred money that was collected at a humanitarian concert for Tijana; a girl from Montenegro who was soon going for surgery; a girl from Tuzla who was traveling to Vienna for surgery; a guy from Zagreb and dozens of people from the area suddenly started getting money from all parts of ex-Yugoslavia. All the people who joined in to help others were happy too, especially Sergej and me of course, getting this incredible opportunity to be a part of it all, as if by a miracle.

* * *

I was helping an Orthodox child and the threats from Muslim nationalists were getting so sick that the police sped up the process of issuing me a gun permit. So I started carrying, albeit unwillingly.

Every morning, if I was to take the car somewhere, I'd first look under it to see if there were any explosives planted. I took our names off the post-box and the doorbell. Amra was in a state of panic. I was cool about it, saying that dangerous people don't make threats like that as they leave traces on the internet but that didn't mean there were no individuals or groups preparing something in silence.

* * *

One of the people who wanted to help was Eldin. He asked me to come personally to collect the money.

"The director is expecting you. Third floor, door to the right," the receptionist said. In the meeting room, I met Eldin.

"Fedja, thank you for coming," he said warmly and continued. "I see you are doing great things and I wanted to join. This building you came into is a is a sort of a research institute. In the basement, there is a bunker for testing explosives, you'll see it later. During the war I was a member of a kind of, well let's say, a special unit and today I am heading this institute that not many people know about. I'd like to tell you something. The people who gave me this position did so to put me out of the way. I know too many things I shouldn't know. Those people are capable of doing things that you wouldn't believe anyone is capable of doing. I know you were in a special unit too during the war. I know you were in front of the parliament when it all started. You saw then that snipers shot at people from the Holiday Inn Hotel. Did you ever wonder why those snipers were never caught? A man with your military experience should know how easy it is to catch a sniper inside a building. You surround the building, close it off and then search room by room, while others are watching for anyone coming in or out. When you find the suspects, you take them in and find out if they are snipers or not. Right? Still, remember they were never caught. Is there anything suspicious about that? People have died in this country in different ways and in the papers it said they died of heart attacks, suicides, traffic accidents or some other accidental death. A pathologist placed there by the party to write false autopsy reports, people killed without anyone knowing, not even their families. The people you are attacking are dangerous and I am afraid you won't survive. I am telling you this not as a threat but as friendly advice."

After the chat we went to see the bunker for explosives, he gave me some money for the guy who needed the lung transplant, we said our goodbyes and I left. It didn't sound like a conspiracy theory to me. I think I can tell, with great certainty, when someone is lying. I have a degree in that area.

I had touched the hornet's nest and now they were pissed at me. I couldn't give a fuck, I am pissed off as well and I won't stop. I didn't fight for a country like this and I will not give it up without a single shot. I have a right to all of this just as much as they do.

Then the trench warfare begun. Eye to eye. Me against three million nationalists. They tried and tested all sorts of methods but they didn't silence me. Disgustingly, using the methods of Goebbels as only fascists can, they tried to sell this as a news story to the media:

"ACTOR FEDJA STUKAN BEAT UP HIS THREE-AND-A-HALF-YEAR-OLD DAUGHTER.

Famous Sarajevo actor Fedja Stukan (39), has beaten up his 3.5 year old daughter. Just before 4pm, an unknown person called the operational centre of the Ministry of the Interior for Sarajevo Canton, to tell them that a male had physically attacked an underaged child in Mehmed Spaho Street. After arriving at the scene, the police arrested Fedja Stukan at his address, in a building known as Parkusa. As reported by eye-witnesses, the male in question is the famous Sarajevo actor Fedja Stukan, who was visibly drunk and first had a verbal fight with his wife and then, in front of other people, struck his underaged daughter a number of times and continued to do so once back in his apartment. After the arrival of police and ambulance, eyewitnesses said that the young person, escorted by an older female, was taken by ambulance.

We contacted the spokesperson of the University of Sarajevo Clinical Centre, Biljana Jandrić, and she confirmed that a young child, escorted by one of the members of the mother's family, was brought to the hospital as a result of domestic violence but didn't want to give any further information."

Even some ultra-right-wing websites condemned this move. It was too much, even for them. When this attempt failed, they then began to paste this text under every article on every news portal in the country. Judging by the amount of hate in the comments, it was easy to work out that my death was what nationalists of all three confessions wanted most. I called my friend Admir, who had a news website and asked him to place a fake news article that I'd died. I first told my friends and family what I intend to do.

* * *

"We have learnt from reliable sources, that body of famous BiH actor, Fedja Stukan, was discovered by his wife at 10:00hrs this morning in their bathroom. Police suspect it is a case of overdose."

This news spread with the speed of light. The nationalists were crazed with happiness and openly jubilant on websites and Facebook profiles. But as I had planned, their happiness was short-lived.

I can't lie and say that all the religious leaders in my country were bad and against me. Bugari, an imam and hafiz (one who knows the Qur'an by heart), saw me in his library. Krepo had arranged the meeting secretly, so no one else had seen me. When we met in front of his mosque, he told me:

"Fedja, I can't believe I am meeting you. I am very happy. I follow your Facebook and online posts and everything you are saying about religion, it is all true."

I didn't expect this kind of meeting and I was completely caught off guard. He had all the relevant authors in the field of philosophy in his library. I came to see him with one idea. I read an interesting interview with an Orthodox priest Chrysostomos, a truly well-intended charismatic man, who like Bugari, instead of being a head of his religious community, was thrown to the periphery so he wouldn't progressively influence a larger number of believers. My idea was that Chrysostomos, Bugari and myself go for a coffee together. It would usually be unheard of for two such figures to meet. Bugari really liked this idea and he sent me an email:

"Thank you for your effort and this rare wish! I hope we will be drinking coffee more often with such open and tolerant people, the kind that we are in shortage

of. Thank you once more. See you in beauty and peace!

Bugari."

And then I sent a letter to Chrysostomos:

"Dear Father Chrysostomos, I hope this letter finds you in good mood and even better health.

My name is Fedja Stukan. I am a pilot, a parachutist and a graduate of the Academy of Performing Arts in Sarajevo. I am an atheist by religion but that in no way diminishes my admiration for you, your work, and your words that I had a chance to read on the Buka website.

"I have to admit you have awoken my hope, a hope that has been dormant for ages, a hope that people such as yourself exist at all and especially in this region. I actually met another great man today, enriching my life by his acquaintance and I became overwhelmed by a wish to address you as a human to human, in the hope that you will have time to read this letter carefully.

"I was born in Sarajevo, into a mixed marriage. I fought in the Army of BiH, but today I have a lot of friends who were RS Army soldiers, HVO[16] and

---

16 HVO – One of three sides in the BiH war. HVO – "the regular" army of the para-state called Herceg-Bosna, were renown for concentration camps, expulsions and killings of non-Catholics. The founders of Herceg-Bosna have been sentenced to long prison terms in a court in The Hague for a joint criminal enterprise.

HOS[17]. I am an active member of the Banja Luka parachute club and have a number of friends from all sides there with whom I have daily contact.

"Your interview made me think that you also don't believe that the future of this country lies in conflict and divisions. All of us were witnesses to the political manipulation of faith and religion, still happening today and I believe you, as a priest are particularly disturbed by this. Religion, like anything else, has become a tool for achieving the political aims of people who are deeply involved in criminal activities.

"Like yourself, I am trying to make life better in my own way, trying to get people to do good deeds and acting so to serve as a model.

"Part of my life I spent as a homeless refugee and today I am trying to help the homeless. Sometimes I succeed but mostly I don't. When I read an interview where you said that inter-religious relations have stopped and that only rarely they send a greeting to one another or good wishes for each other's holidays, I got an idea that I would wholeheartedly want to materialise. You can call it Utopian but the hope you have given me with your humane and sincere words, has opened new horizons for me, horizons I would like to aim towards as a human being.

"There is a hafiz, Bugari in Sarajevo, you have probably heard of him. The progressive position of Mr. Bugari in propagating reconciliation, peace and

---

17 HOS – similar like HVO

tolerance is incredibly similar to yours and mine as well."

After this pleasant introduction, I told him of my idea and wish that we, people with all our differences and different convictions, can still be just humans and that as such, we could get together and have a coffee. Without any talk of politics, we could just sit down and have a relaxed coffee, like normal human beings.

Whether that would be in public or not, I leave up to you to decide. It is simply much more important that we start talking and spending time together. To show that, we should just simply start talking to one another, outside the politics. And as you say, sharing things we have in common, things that connect us, and not just those that distance and divide us. And maybe, with such a bright example, we could take on the monopoly politicians have over our happiness and unhappiness and finally let spiritual people be the true leaders to promote tolerance and coexistence and spread the real message of religion; love. With that, we'd prove that politics does not rule the human spirit and that it cannot stand in the path of the good, smart and well-intended people who don't see materialism as their only worldly fulfilment.

"Mr. Bugari has accepted my invitation without hesitation and with overt happiness, enthusiasm and impatience for this and future meetings to be in friendship and peace, and for them to be fruitful.

Dear Father Chrysostomos, we will be awaiting your response with great anticipation, hoping you will find time for this friendly and well-intended get together.

With sincere and deep respect, Fedja Stukan

Sent from my iPhone"

And soon I got a reply;

"Dear Fedja, thank you for getting in touch. I read your letter with great interest. I am glad that you have seen my interview, albeit recorded a while back. I have understood your wish to meet. I would be delighted to host you at my place in Bosanski Petrovac. I gladly have coffee, lunch, celebrate Saint patron days, Christmas, Easter and Eid with my Muslim neighbours equally as I do with Serbs. I am often in Bihać and other places, meeting with people, talking and discussing different topics, etc. Unfortunately to all decent people, international and inter-religious relations have been contaminated so much, that my idea itself has been condemned and rejected. It is a tragedy, but each needs to fight in their own community by setting good examples. I was in Sarajevo few days ago and I felt the atmosphere of heavily distorted relationships. Parents, the clergy and the people themselves are to blame for that. Politicians use those and similar devices to win favours and votes.

It is manipulation of the people who are spiritually suffering. But this is an image of poor Bosnia being torn apart by those who believe they have the monopoly over it.

Greetings, Chrysostomos."

Unfortunately the meeting never happened. Bugari eventually left BiH and went to Montenegro, where his brains, honesty and benevolence were more appreciated. And Father Chrysostomos went on to fill the position of a disgraced priest who was caught on video committing various sexual acts but co-incidentally lost the ability to speak and so could not comment on it or be brought to justice.

* * *

I got a text on my phone from Sergej, "Tijana has died!"

* * *

I had not played a single role at the Chamber Theatre where I was employed, for a few years now and I was a bit embarrassed for receiving a salary and doing nothing. The theatre director Dragan, told me that a new play would soon be on, directed by Sulejman, a director that I hadn't been talking to for years as he unjustly replaced me in one of his plays. He begged me to make up with him but that was a bit silly as we had had a conflict that ended up in the media, so it wasn't easy to sort out. One evening I was flipping the channels and I saw Sulejman as a guest on a TV show, so I called in and introduced myself and said that although I never agreed with him over anything, that I agree with everything he said tonight. Although I didn't know what he'd said, it was a good way to make up and I was promised a part. When I found out what play and lines I had to do, I got really depressed. It was about the genocide and there were a bunch of Chetniks in the scene harassing a guy throughout the play and I was to play one of the Chetniks. It was a totally irrelevant role and if it was taken out no one would have noticed. I can't play a fucking Chetnik, and I can't put the Chetniks' destruction together with the performing arts. Those are two total opposites for me. Every single atom in my being was against it but I couldn't get out if it. Or maybe I could? Sure I can! I have an ace up my sleeve, I have hepatitis C!

First thing in the morning I went to the clinic for infectious diseases and I said, "I have to get a treatment right away."

"Fine, but you have to have a biopsy first."

"Cool. Let's get it done right away."

The doctor cleaned a spot between my ribs with a cotton pad soaked in alcohol, gave me a local anaesthetic, stuck a biopsy needle in, took it out and said, "There you are!"

I said, "What's that?"

"Well, it's all done!"

"Done?"

"Yes, done!"

"I can't believe that's that. I've been avoiding the biopsy for years, and it's taken two and a half seconds and I didn't feel a thing."

"Well, I told you before this is routine procedure and you wouldn't feel it!"

"When can I start the treatment?"

"As soon as we get the results back."

I spent that night in the hospital, in case anything went wrong. Hospitals always get me thinking. I've spent so much time in them already. In the evening, I went to the balcony on the first floor of the Clinic for Infectious Diseases to have a cigarette. Just across from where I was standing was the psychiatric ward where I'd spent time twenty years before. There was a street between us, some twenty metres wide. The window to the 'glass room' was on the ground floor and I couldn't see the legs of a nurse in white clogs, walking down the poorly lit corridor. Everyone was getting ready for their evening medication. Then I saw the legs of some crazy guy, barely being dragged and then the others left, walking in the opposite direction. Maybe it's Jozo, he must still be there. I know exactly what it's like in there. If I focus, I can still smell the stench.

It would be difficult to count the number of times I was close to death. Not just close to death even, I was dead several times. If I took into consideration the number of second chances I'd already had, the chance of yet another one was quite slim. Considering how long I'd been carrying the disease, my liver sample results were not going to be promising. Blood tests confirmed that I had a few million more replicated viruses per cubic millimetre than any patient they had treated for hepatitis so far. I remember how I got it. We were sitting in Dimension's room and he was trying to inject but as usual, it was taking hours. We had one syringe and I was waiting for my turn. In an open drawer I saw a thick needle with a blood clot that looked like a blob of fat red jelly. I took the gear, removed the blood clot, cooked and shot up.

"Now you have hepatitis C!", he said, more as information than anything else and without emotion. That was the first time I had heard of the disease and due to the level manner in which he had made the statement, I concluded it was not too dangerous.

"I got it from the time I was shooting up with EKV[18]".

---

18 The cult band from Belgrade. The simbol of the urban, educated youth, that were openly against the war. All but a few drummers died during the nineties from AIDS and Hepatitis C.

OK whatever, I thought, all drugged up. If he had told me AIDS was in that syringe, I would have shot up with the same ease anyway.

* * *

The day after, when I was discharged, I went to the psychiatry building to see if there was still a hole from the armour-piercing shell that killed Drago. I never saw it from the outside and you wouldn't believe it, things are still as they were then. A hole of fifteen centimetres in diameter, patched up some twenty years ago. I came up close and touched the plaster, thinking how something so small could cause so much damage on the inside.

* * *

Emir returned from New York in style. First he was in his hometown of Prijedor in western BiH, where the Orthodox in 1992 had ordered Muslims to wear white bands on their arms and mark their houses with white sheets. Then their neighbours and friends took them to concentration camps and killed them. Amongst more than three thousand civilians there were 102 children. A large number of people were slaughtered with a knife or beaten to death, some were shot and others thrown off a cliff into the abyss below and then beheaded just for pure pleasure. In the end, they all ended up in mass graves. Then they used excavators and trucks to move bodies to secondary, and then third mass graves, trying to hide their crime. Imagine the amount of manpower and machinery needed to move thousands of bodies from a few hundred mass graves with excavators and trucks and move them from one mass grave to another. Convoys of excavators and trucks. Hundreds and hundreds of 'workers'. What was the budget for all of that? Who approved it? It couldn't have been cheap. The monsters who organised, ordered and implemented all this are idols to the orthodox believers in Republika Srpska. The Orthodox church has pronounced them saints. I wonder what kind of amoeba you have to be, to look up to the worst of civilisation's filth?

* * *

Emir set up an art installation in Prijedor; he stood in the main town square with a white armband on his sleeve. After the installation, he was a hero to Muslims, until he was filmed eating pork and the recording of him was published. That is when they started hating him. They called for him to be killed. It is hard for me to understand that some people can split atoms and others can only split logs.

* * *

After this installation, Refik, myself and the rest of our crew posted photos of ourselves with a white armband on our sleeves as a sign of support and that went viral across the country the same day. Since then, the White Armband Day has become traditional. Each 31st May, people on Facebook post their profile photos with a white armband on their sleeve.

* * *

A few days later, my medical report came back. My whole liver had 25% fibrosis with its function reduced by the same amount. I went to work and told the director I had to get treatment as soon as possible and that it was probable I'd be feeling depressed, experience weakness, loss of hair, and who knows what else. I said that it would be better if I didn't start a project I might not be able to complete due to medical reasons. He agreed with me.

* * *

The therapy started and seemed OK. I felt a loss of appetite and lost some weight. I often felt weak but not depressed and had no psychological side effects. On the contrary, I felt great.

＊ ＊ ＊

I started doing activities and installations with Emir as we agreed in New York. The first activity was his idea. We should visit all the concentration camps in the country from the last war, those run by the Orthodox, then those run by Catholics and then those run by Muslims. In each of them, civilians of the other two faiths were killed and raped. We visited them and paid our respects to all the victims.

Then we put up one of my installations. We hung a huge Bosnian flag from one of the tallest buildings in Sarajevo. That wouldn't have been a problem was it not for the fact that it was the old flag of the former Socialist Republic of BiH, when the country was part of Yugoslavia. The nationalists took it quite hard. The day after, the same flag was flying in the 'enemy' territories; 'West' Mostar and Banja Luka.

Then again one of Emir's; we got a few busloads of people of good will and took a walk together through Prijedor, laid flowers at the main square and asked the authorities to permit the erection of a monument to the murdered children of Prijedor. This they couldn't allow, as to do so would mean admitting what they'd done, crimes they had been denying. The walk through Prijedor and laying of flowers at the square became a tradition as well.

Then one of my ideas again. We painted over a huge chessboard coat of arms in a small Bosnian city and made it into an image of a heart. We called the installation, 'Let's make love, not play Chess'.

The Catholics had drawn the Croatian coat of arms in that part of BiH territory to provoke the Muslims there. We did similar installations across the country. Wherever Catholics are in a majority (and they often are because they have ethnically cleansed the territory by displacement and mass killings) they put up Croat instead of BiH flags. Catholics and Orthodox erect huge crosses on the hills to annoy Muslims and Muslims build mosques which then play loud calls for prayer at around 120dB. This is the way tribes scare each other, letting the others know they are not welcome on their territory. Hyper-production of places of worship serves to mark the territory. The game is similar to Monopoly, only with live people and lots of death.

* * *

Then someone posted a link on my wall saying, "A little girl called Belmina can't leave the country for medical treatment due to problems with her being issued a passport!"

The problem was this, every person in BiH has a JMBG or unique citizen identification number. The Orthodox were asking for the last two numbers of their JMBG to identify their faith of origin, however the Muslims wanted the numbers to be the same for everyone.

As usual, they couldn't agree. For a year. This was a serious problem in my country and was the reason why no child born here in the last year had been given a JMBG. Without the number, you can't get a passport, so you can't go to the seaside outside of the country and you can't go to have medical treatment abroad. Belmina was dying and she urgently needed a treatment unavailable in this failure of a country and the passport problem was so large that it couldn't be resolved in a short period of time.

* * *

BiH is the only country in the world that has three presidents: one Muslim, elected by Muslims; one Catholic, elected by Catholics; and one Orthodox, elected by the Orthodox.

The wife of the Muslim president (who is the son of the former president), is a doctor. Her husband, almost by force, installed her as the director of the biggest hospital in the country. The health system, like all the systems here, is totally destroyed. Patients are buying medication and bandages themselves, as hospitals often don't have even the basics. Money meant for healthcare ends up in the pockets of the members of the ruling party, which was the aim of her instalment as the director of this institution. Doctors were on the streets protesting about it for a while but they were fired one by one, so the rebellion was suffocated. Whoever dared to speak up or say anything on the subject was immediately fired and replaced by incompetent party members, some with bought and forged university diplomas. That's why parents are trying to move their sick children anywhere out of here for treatment.

* * *

At first, this day was like any other. Aya and I saw Amra off to work. I was trying to have my coffee but it was a difficult task, as Aya was pulling my arm. "Daddy, Daddy, let's play with Play-Doh". We were making some silly shapes: worms and star-shaped worms. Aya made a Play-Doh blob and then gave it a name, we laughed and kissed. It was an ordinary day. Then I saw an article again about the sick girl Belmina without her JMBG number. I was angry but hid it from Aya. I wasn't worried about her, she had a passport. I was still smiling but inside I was cursing everyone in that parliament and anyone who voted for them. I felt I had to do something but I had no idea what. At 11am the phone rings. It's Duca.

"Bro, are we going to do something?"

"Yes but what?"

"I don't know, maybe use our cars to block the parliament building?"

"When, where?"

"The parliament session starts at 12.30pm, I'll see you at the parking lot near the carwash in Kotromanića street at 12.45."

"Aya my love, Daddy has to go to a protest."

"I want to go to protest as well."

My darling wants to go to protest. She is Daddy's girl!

"You'll come with your mummy later, now you are going to Romana's."

"But I want to go to the protest!"

I arrived in front of the carwash at 12.45 and met many people I didn't know.

"Šemso-Fedja... Dalibor-Fedja... etc". I greeted my new friends warmly and asked, "What's the plan?"

"Hmmm, the plan is... do we have a plan? We don't have a plan."

"OK," I said, "Give me a piece of paper and a pen."

Aida passed me a colouring pen and a copy of a flyer with Belmina's photo. I flipped it over and on the other side, I drew the streets around the Parliament building.

"Zoka and Duca, you go first with your cars and park in both lanes. Aldin and I will follow with our cars and we'll stop right in front of the building entrance. Darko and Tijana, Boris and Zlaja, Šemso and Dalibor, you park behind us, we'll get out of the cars, we'll lock them up and wait for a traffic jam to clog the street. We will wait for the police and then... I don't know, something will happen!"

We all gathered around the piece of paper, looking at it, thinking, making suggestions, laughing and finally agreeing on the plan. Adrenaline was rushing. I look at my watch. It was 12.59.

"Let's go people!"

We gave each other one more look of insecurity and we moved to the cars. On the way to the car I posted on my Facebook; "Everyone in front of the Parliament, now!"

I got into my car, we formed into a small convoy and off we went.

As we turned into the street to the right, my heart sped up, let's go! Zoka parked his car in the right lane and got out. Duca waited for a car to pass from the opposite direction and then crossed into his lane and parked. I stopped my car at the building entrance. All was going to plan. I locked the car, got out and looked around me. Everyone was in their positions, we'd stopped the traffic and as people in their cars began beeping their horns, we waited. The first police patrol arrived with flashing lights and called for back-up. Very professionally, they re-directed the traffic and very soon the street was completely empty. It was now only our cars parked where they were and us, with our fingers up our arses, clueless as to what to do next.

Slowly, people were joining us, soon there were fifty of us. People we knew from different events, from theatre and cinema, always the same people. A tow-truck came but we surrounded the cars and wouldn't let them get towed. They gave up.

Šemso stepped up on a car and started screaming into a megaphone. He was brilliant at it. With a pinch of humour, he was nailing it directly. He knew the issue, he showed no respect to those up there and I liked it. Šemso is made for this kind of thing and I had no intention of interfering. More people arrived and security started to increase.

Duca played Dubioza Kolektiv[19] in the car and the atmosphere became tolerable, it became excellent actually. The media started to arrive. We were maintaining good relations with the police and security. They understood why we were doing it and secretly, they supported us. A woman escorted by bodyguards came out of the building and walked towards us, as the media surrounded her. She told us that a temporary decision had been made. Šemso told her via megaphone that we were not satisfied and we would stay until they passed a law at state level. The woman left. I saw there weren't enough

---

19 Most famous music band from BiH, with a powerful lyrics about social inequality and injustice.

of us to change anything. I was wondering whether it might have been better to have left after the decision. We did what we needed to do, Belmina would get her JMBG and be able to travel for treatment. We had won, we proved that things could be done when there is a will, we helped a child and scored. What were we still doing here then?

As members of Parliament were leaving the building, we whistled at them and passed comments, but we were humorous and well mannered. I saw few people still supporting us, I had expected more, at least the parents of children without a JMBG, but only two couples came. Belmina's mother arrived and made a statement for the cameras. I had a lump in my throat and could feel tears in my eyes but my dark glasses were good camouflage. With all the problems she was facing, did she need to deal with all this political shit as well?

We agreed on the next steps, whether to stay or to leave? We decided to set new protests at 10am the next day. In the meantime, we stayed.

The media reported that we were still there, so friends brought us blankets, coffee, juice, and food that we shared with the security and police. It was a nice, friendly atmosphere. Amra and Aya came as well and we ran around the grass, chasing each other and laughing. Then the night came.

After a while people slowly began to disperse and we, who had initially blocked the building, stayed.

I got into my car, pushed the seat back and tried to sleep unsuccessfully. I was not hopeful about the protest tomorrow. I was convinced no-one would come. Every hour or so, I took a photo and posted it on Facebook, just so people knew what was going on.

Dawn came and by then it was twenty-four hours since I had slept, even for a second. We slowly got out of our cars and waited. The sun rose. There was no-one on the square but us. People were slowly coming to work in the Parliament, they passed by us, looking at us like we were some kind of losers, and kept walking. I was still posting photos. A few TV cameras came but no one was taking it too seriously, least of all me. Members of parliament went in and out. Around 10am, a few couples with kids arrived. They were the reason we were there. That gave me some hope. A few dozen more people came and it seemed to me there were around fifty of us. I took more photos and kept posting them. Two hundred people. Slowly, I was becoming certain that something was happening. Šemso took the megaphone again and began talking. People were reacting, they were angry at the members of parliament, at the state, at everything really. There were a thousand of us by this point. People were coming up to me, taking photos and posting them too. The word was spreading and the crowds were getting bigger, now two thousand. The members of parliament were starting to panic as the situation became uncomfortable. The TV crews were there, every single one that there was, local and foreign. They came up to me and I screamed into the cameras, "Either get off your asses and come here or sit at home and watch children die!"

A Serbian parliamentary representative – a woman – tweeted, "We are surrounded. The protesters are shouting anti-Serb slogans!" Had I not known that out of the ten people who started all of this, five of them were Serbs, maybe I would have believed her. Now three thousand. Some of the members of parliament were trying to escape and people were asking me if they should let them. I told them that no-one is to leave the building and since the building has a number of exits and low windows, I suggested we form a chain, that we hold hands and fully surround the building, as there were now so many of us that it was easily possible. We created a large, impenetrable ring around the building. Four thousand.

The parliament sent people among us to try to break the circle by spreading rumors that the building had a secret underground tunnel with an exit a few hundred metres away, and that the members of parliament were using it right at that moment. I could see a part of the ring collapsing. I called a girl I knew who'd worked in the building for years and asked her if there was a tunnel; she said no. I ran after people telling them there was no tunnel and that they should go back to their positions. A few of my friends on bikes joined us and I asked them to go in front of the garage entrance on the side as that was our weakest spot. If members of parliament tried to leave in their cars, people would get scared and move, which would enable the members' escape. Suddenly, there were thirty bikers parking in front of the garage, totally blocking it.

Vans carrying special police were arriving and things seemed to be getting out of control. I was nearly exhausted. For the last few hours, I'd been running around the building without a break and sometimes I would lose consciousness for a moment and quickly regain it again. This was now top news across the world as well. Special units were between us and the building and mothers with children in pushchairs were tightening the ring around them, leaving them helpless. The police from different units argued about who was responsible for which part of the square.

"You are responsible all the way up to this step!"

"No, that is the Canton police jurisdiction!"

"No, not us. It is the building security!"

"No, you are!"

"No, not us!"

"Yes, you..." It was like a scene from a cartoon.

No one knew what was going on and the situation started to remind me of Mad Max. There were now different characters and organisations trying to use the situation to serve their own purposes, radicals trying to take over the protest. They were presenting it as their own protests, on their on-line profiles and to their followers. Five thousand. Football fans were joining us. The noise of whistles was deafening. Someone was saying they could smell petrol and that someone wanted to burn the building with more than 2,500 people working inside it. Politicians in the media called us terrorists, while the foreign embassies told them it was not terrorism but democracy. Meanwhile the Serbs in the building were still chanting that it was all directed against them, as usual.

I got a call from the US Embassy to tell me that they were carefully following the situation and that in case any of the organisers get arrested, they would raise it to a higher diplomatic level, that they were by our side as long as our protests were peaceful and democratic. The British Embassy supported us too. They sent me a text saying that, if I had time, come to the ambassador's residence tomorrow. CNN was calling me for an interview, Al Jazeera, the Washington Post, the New York Times. At around three in the afternoon, the members of parliament finally called on the organisers to negotiate. We'll negotiate. Darko, Tijana, Zoka, Šemso and myself; this was decided by the people in front of the Parliament and four of them were already inside. Escorted by police and security in large numbers, I walked through the crowd. Before I went in, I said to those gathered that, if I am not back in forty-five minutes, that means I've been taken hostage, and then... I don't know what then.

That scenario was not unrealistic, as we were entering the mafia headquarters, going among those who were not unfamiliar with executions in order to achieve their goals. The only thing preventing them from resolving this their own way was the large number of local and foreign media whom they'd been trying to convince that they are democrats for decades. That's the line they'd been using to get the money from European and world-wide funds, which they then successfully stole. And it wouldn't be good for them to be left without that income as that was the sole reason for them being there.

I entered the building, emptied my pockets at the entrance and placed the contents in a plastic box that then went through an X-ray machine, similar to the ones at the airport. Behind the machine, there were some twenty low ranking ass-kissers, hiding. They were in a state of panic. I passed through security and entered the main hall where a debate was taking place. There were still four big guys in dark suits with an earpiece in their ear around me, taking me through the crowd as the murmuring stopped. Silence. The crowd slowly moved in absolute silence, to let us pass through. I couldn't help but notice how all those who were about to take a bite of the scampi canapes or sip their drink, remained with their mouths open while watching me walk down that big hall. And their eyes were saying, "Is my fate dependent on this jerk wearing ripped All-Stars? Is this why I got a degree (or bought one)?"

Some of them came up to me, brown-nosing and discreetly walking alongside our small five-person procession, so the others couldn't hear them saying, "Hey, Fedja, kudos to you for this. I am with you but could you let me out in about an hour, please? I have to get my kid from school."

All that with a pretend sad facial expression that was supposed to make me sympathise or something. I passed by without responding and thought to myself, "Sure, I'll let you go get your kid but only when you let other kids get medical treatment."

As we got into the elevator, they were still looking at us with their mouths wide open. They probably bit into the scampi as soon as the door closed and tried to be cool as if nothing was happening. They'd get to go home after the negotiations anyway. Or at least they hoped so. Hope is the last to die.

We went to the chairman's office. Him and few of his cronies were sitting at a large round table. Zoka, Šemso, Darko and Tijana were already there.

"This is turning into a hostage crisis. You know we can lock you up for this?" he said.

"You are in no position to make threats," I replied, while taking a seat at the table.

"The Serbs have locked themselves in their office and are calling special units to come and rescue them from the building. The special police is ready with armoured vehicles at Vrace, just waiting for the order to go. You are risking being the initiators of a new armed conflict in the country! When you get out, tell those people to let us go. Besides us, there are around three hundred foreign bankers and investors in the building who should not be seeing this situation. We will lose a lot of donations because of you. Bosnia could face an unimaginable crisis."

"In case you haven't noticed, this country is already in an unimaginable crisis and has been for a couple of decades now. We are asking you to sit at the table and agree today to pass the Law on JMBG at state level. You have the ability, since no one has left the building. We weren't aware of the bankers but now that we know, we think it is even better because we hope we've interfered with at least some of your thieving plans and we are glad we've shown those people how you run this country. Stop scaring us with the special police in armoured vehicles. If there needs to be a war, let it be, because a country shouldn't exist like this and if war is the only way to change something, so be it. Look at the situation in front of the building, no one is controlling the crowds of people and it is slowly losing control. We are doing our best to prevent this becoming a huge tragedy."

The discussion continued but they simply didn't want to do anything on the issue. The crowd was chanting my name outside as the forty-five minute deadline was coming near.

"Try to talk some sense in them, please," were his last words.

"No guarantees, but we'll do our best."

As the security took us back the same way, I couldn't help but notice that those in the hall were still in the stop-frame, with their mouths wide open in silence.

I exited the building and instead of turning to the right, where the bunch of journalists were waiting, I turned left to buy time. My head was in complete chaos. I moved slowly through the crowd towards the journalists.

A couple of million people in front of their TVs are waiting for me to make a statement and I don't know what to say. It is clear to me that I can end all this and release the bankers and parliamentarians if I say that an agreement has been reached but then I would risk the masses thinking I was paid to end all this. If not that, then we risk continuing which really could have unthinkable consequences.

By chance, I have just become a leader of some new movement. Someone who could change the future of the country and whatever I say, it will change history. I am dizzy with all this responsibility, the hepatitis medication I was taking and the lack of sleep. I slowly come closer to the cameras. There is a sense of jubilation as I am holding the state mafia by the neck but if I decide to stay in front of the parliament... the consequences will be all my fault. I don't know what to do. Cameramen are already putting cameras on their shoulders and starting to record. Dozens of mics of different colours are directed at me. I stand in front of them... and say nothing. I don't know what to say. After an eternity of silence, totally spontaneously, I say, *"Nothing was agreed, we are staying here!"*

Huge applause breaks out, the sound of hundreds of whistles continue the noise. If only I could get half an hour's sleep.

I followed the posts on Facebook. We were getting support from people in Republika Srpska for the first time ever. People from all sides could see that the protests had no religious background. It was clear that we were there only because of the children. We expanded the list of demands and now we wanted to force them to resolve a number of issues that realistically could be resolved in five minutes. They asked us to let food be delivered into the building as they had eaten all the scampi. We let the food pass. We're not savages. We didn't want to mistreat anyone, not even that worthless bunch of criminals.

The politicians were trying to present all of this as a political game of the opposition and they used their media and fake news. It was more than obvious that no-one believed them anymore. They said we were being paid by Soros, Turkey, Saudi Arabia, the USA and UK, but nothing worked. Famous artists from all parts of ex-Yugoslavia were posting messages of support on their profiles. Protests spread to other cities in BiH. Something beautiful was happening. Aya and Amra were there, we were running around on the grass, chasing each other again.

Night came. It was more than forty hours since I slept. My brain was slowly shutting down and I'd already missed the ground under my feet a few times. I fell on my knees and hit the asphalt. Around 11pm I told someone on the team that I had to go home for an hour, I lived just 500 metres away. I needed to finally have a shower, change and have something to eat. If there was any trouble, I'd be there in a second. As soon as I sat at the table, the phone rang.

"Hello?"

It was my friend Elvir, calling to say, "Hey, where are you? I got to the front of the Parliament and there's no one here, just your car parked in front!"

"What?" I looked at my watch. 3am. WTF?

I went to the Parliament and yes, no one was there. I got into my car and drove home. I lay down and fell asleep.

As soon as I woke up, I called Šemso. He said that he was in front of the parliament, so I went there with Aya and found him. About a dozen people were with him.

"What happened last night?" I asked. He told me that people started to disperse around midnight. They were hungry and tired, and nobody came to replace them. The special police used that moment to create a corridor and took all the people out of the building. And that was it. There weren't enough people to stop it. There were few incidents, a few people were arrested but they were released in the morning.

"So, what's the plan?" I asked.

"Plan? Aaaaah, a plan? Do we have a plan? No, we don't have a plan. Do you have one?"

"Nope!"

People came up to us to take photos, to greet and congratulate us. We were now world-wide famous. Washington Post, New York Times, CNN, BBC... we were top news across the globe.

While we sat in the shade in front of the parliament building, thinking what to do next, we were looking at the news online, reading comments out loud and laughing at nationalist conspiracy theories and some of the rubbish they were writing about us. People had been gathering in Sofia in front of the parliament since early that morning, they were forming a ring around the building. We were glad they are stealing our moves. Facebook was full of support. Supporting protests soon started in all the cities of BiH, even people from RS[20] were coming out in the streets in their cities. Actors and musicians from Serbia were taking photos with a white paper on their chest with JMBG written on it and posting photos on their and my Facebook walls.

The whole world was supporting us. Children of all skin colours, religions and nations sent in video messages in all the different languages of the world. It was beautiful.

TV crews arrived again, setting up their tripods. People assembled again. Drivers driving past honked their horns in support. Members of the Dubioza Kolektiv band came to see us and we agreed for them to have a concert there the following day.

New news on the net: "Three-month-old baby girl Berina in critical condition. Turned back from the border crossing due to not having a passport". An ambulance had tried to take her to Belgrade for surgery, but the border police didn't let them through. An hour after we found this out, her parents came to the Parliament and stood in front of the press cameras to give details.

20 'Republika Srpska' – Serbian Republic

It was so frustrating. Berina was in a very bad state and would die unless something was done urgently. Suddenly, students appeared in front of the building. Thousands of them. Then workers. A deafening sound of whistles and car horns. Taxi drivers blocked the intersections, causing a total traffic jam across the city. The atmosphere was great. There was none of the tension of the day before. In the evening, a parliamentary spokesperson came with a paper to say that a decision had finally been made!

But it was too late for Berina, unfortunately. She just became another victim, among many others, of this dysfunctional nationalist state. She became a statistic.

* * *

Upon invitation, I went to a reception at the British Ambassador's residence. At the entrance to the huge courtyard packed with guests, I was greeted by two security guards in suits and a waiter wearing white gloves, who gestured to me to come into the garden. As I slowly approached the guests, I noticed a commotion. An applause started but I couldn't see who they were applauding yet. The applause turned into an ovation and I noticed that their heads were turned in my direction. I actually turned to look behind me to see if a famous politician had come in after me. No-one. The waiter and the security behind me were also clapping. WTF? As I came nearer the crowd of guests, I realised they were applauding me and that it wasn't ceasing but instead, was picking up.

The British Ambassador said into a microphone, "Here he is at last! He came in the end. Fedja, I hope that you haven't surrounded us and that you'll let the people go home when this party is over, because who'd put up with a crowd as horrible as this for a few days? If you want to take some diplomats hostage, I suggest you surround the house next door. The Pakistani ambassador lives there, they have much better food...". We all laughed.

Soon the secretaries of high foreign dignitaries started coming up to me, telling me their bosses would like to meet me too. OK, let them come. The High Representative for BiH, the Head of the UN Mission, NATO and more. Out of our own important ones, I met the chief prosecutor, who was later charged for corruption but will never be held to account of course. Five of us stepped aside and started a serious talk. I can't say that I was up to it. I can't say that I would ever engage in politics as that would mean sitting in an office, shaking hands with nationalists and being surrounded by a whole lot of yes-men. But I can say with certainty that at that moment I was the most important political figure in the country and the only one NATO, UN and the OHR listened to with attention and respect. In just a few steps I had got to the top of the country and if I'd wanted to, I could have stayed there. If I had political ambition, this country could look totally different today. We will never know.

* * *

Belmina, the other little girl died.

* * *

Some of the Bosnian intellectuals who didn't join us in the protests started spreading conspiracy theories and competed to see who could think up and publish worse filth to discredit us. Since we were the ones who reminded them that things can change if you get up from behind the keyboard. They hated us more than the nationalists did. They said that we were using children for our own pro-motion. I was slowly getting sick of it all. I'd spent twenty-six days in front of the parliament. For what? Self-promotion? Well... fuck you all.

The next step, if there ever is one, will be violent and I don't want to take part in that one. The chil-dren I tried to help – Tijana, Belmina and Berina – are no longer among the living. Maybe it's best if I stop trying to help anyone. I gave it all to try to change something, but it is simply not happening. If I had invested that much energy in myself I could have achieved anything. The things that I've said publicly are all well-known to normal people here, but those that I am trying to convince to continue with their lives and move on don't have the capacity to understand, and that's not something I can change.

* * *

When we got Yugoslavia on its feet to help Tijana, it seemed it was quite fashionable to help sick children. Now no one was paying into anyone's account and my Facebook profile became senseless. People using sick children to make money were getting in touch, as well as the teams abroad that were using these kind of activities to steal millions. They were threatening me as if I'd stepped on their turf to sell drugs, without giving them their cut. I believe I met the worst scum of this planet through charity work. One day I opened the settings on my Facebook to change few options and I saw the Sign Out option. Without planning to do so, I clicked it. It turned out to be one of the smartest moves in my life. I've never gone back to that profile. I've never done an interview or given a statement to local media since (until I wrote this book). I was done with self-promotion.

An interview for my first big job in film production went really well. I'd be producing an American feature film!

* * *

During the filming, new protests started and as I thought, they were violent. All those we managed to calm down and convince not to burn anything were left without anyone to calm them down. A few buildings were burned, the Assembly, the Presidency... honestly, in some perverse way it was nice seeing those buildings in flames, especially the Presidency. The symbol of primitivism and the splitting of the loot between the three faiths. The American Embassy called to ask if I had anything to do with the protests and what the plans were?

"C'mon, please, I'm a pacifist... and a producer! I really have better things to do!"

* * *

During all the rush over the film production, I also went for a casting and got a role in the movie, 'A Perfect Day'.

* * *

After finishing work on the American film, I went to the hospital to get the last shot of my course of Interferon and to do a blood test to see if the treatment had worked. Then I took my small family for three months of filming in Grenada. A week later I got a text from my doctor, "You are cured! Enjoy!"

I certainly will :)

THE END

A few years later, he became a pilot like in his dreams, the real one, with gold stripes on the epaulettes. One day, when he arrived at his new job, he stood on that same escalator, heading to the same upper floor. He barely nodded to greet his colleagues, co-pilots and cabin crew also on their way to the flight. He was trying to hide his emotions, but his heart was beating louder and faster and he could barely catch his breath. In less than an hour, he'd hear "Clear for take-off," through his headset and after that, the force of the propeller would glue him into the seat and raise him high above the clouds and he will watch the sunset from the first row. An airport stewardess rushed to take off the red rope from the pole in front of him and gestured widely with her arm to direct him to skip the queue. In just a few seconds, his whole life flashed before his eyes, all the way up to this point, and his eyes filled with tears.

He saw a cute two or three-year-old boy next to him, holding his mother's hand and looking at him with his eyes wide open.

It's not easy becoming a pilot, he thought to himself. He lowered his glasses further down his nose, looked the child in the eyes and winked; BANG!

That's how it all started!

THE BEGINNING

AYA

My everything. Don't take my path. When the war breaks out – run. Preserving life is the top priority. Nothing is more important. Don't listen to anyone who says anything differently. You get one life only. State and nation are constructs of a very territorial type of monkey and they are nothing else but a synonym for a larger tribe led by a smaller group of monkeys, ready to do literally anything for money. A flag is only a piece of cloth. Anthems are a bunch of sounds and words, so do not give them any deeper meaning. Behind it all are the rich exploiting the poor. Patriotism is for the narrow-minded. The whole world is yours. You have the right to it. Explore it. There is no better way to use time than to travel. Surround yourself with people who appreciate life. Religion is the cult of death; the most morbid human invention and it is there solely for money. Those running it know nothing about life, let alone death. Death is nothing. Death doesn't hurt. Enjoy, that is the essence.

Thank you for being born.

I adore you.

Special thanks to: Angelina Jolie, Brad Pitt, Nađa Štukan, Amra Mehić, Mirna Filipan, Eni Tica, Romana Tica, Radenko Tica, Milan Inđić, Dušanka Inđić, Mustafa Štukan, Vesna Karadžić Štukan, Avdo Štukan, Rabija Štukan, Ema Ruždić, Džemo Ruždić, Zina Ruždić, Amina Ruždić, Hida Mustafić, Jasmina Mustafić, Amir Pandžić, Elma Pandžić, Nađa Pandžić, Sejdalija Mustafić, Nedim Mustafić, Mela Mustafić, Lejla Divović Mustafić, Fatima Oglić, Hamo Oglić, Vedran Tuce, Frankica Tuce, Zlatan Tuce, Ema Tuce, Refik Hodžić, Azra Hodžić, Tarik Hodžić, Salih Hodžić, Emir Hodžić, Sandra Divković, Bojan Divković, Hana Obradović, Ermin Zatega, Selma Poturović Zatega, Luna Zatega, Kan Zatega, Noa Zatega, Nedeljko Kuđeljić, Liam Kuđeljić, Anita Bačić, Aldin Arnautović, Feđa Arnautović, Haris Hadžić, Amina Hadžić, Azra Hadžić, Adnan Hasanbegović, Edin Jahić, Biljana Šerbedžija, Zoran Šerbedžija, Srđan Šerbedžija, Rade Šerbedžija, Lucija Šerbedžija, Nidžara Mehić, Azra Mehić Dolbery, Henry Dolbery, Zijad Mehić, Dea Mehić, Elma Begtašević, Narda Nikšić, Hamdija Salihbegović, Ema Salihbegović, Amira Salihbegović, Zehra Salihbegović, Damir Đurić, Šemsa Đurić, Dragan Đurić, Muamer Đozo, Ajla Ajanović Đozo, Edin Kovač, Amra Pandžo, Mirza Krupalija, Mirsad Krupalija, Nedžad Merdžanović, Jovan Divjak,

Rusmir Efendić, Saša Mandić, Benjamin Zeničanin, Samir Zeničanin, Aida Zeničanin, Melina Alagić, Armin Alagić, Armin Koluder, Suzana Šakotić, Dario Šakotić, Igor Bararon, Mustafa Nadarević, Faruk Jažić, Slaviša Mašić, Mirna Sandžaktarević, Dražen Crnomat, Dario Delibašić, Danko Delibašić, Amir Pašalić, Nenad Dizdarević, Adi Hrustemović, Timur Makarević, Deni Peterković, Ines Mrenica, Simonida Mandić, Sead Pandur, Musatafa Čizmić, Ivor Doder, Dino Ćatović, Domagoj Nižić, Vesna Kenjić, Sanela Pepeljak, Danijela Žutić, Martina Mandek, Mirza Pašić, Adnan Goro, Tina Šmalcelj, Zoran Đaković, Mojca Štrafela, Mirza Hodžić, Stallan Skarsgard, Iva Šimić, Gary Oldman, Anja Kraljević, Vincent Cassel, Adisa Vatreš Selimović, Amar Selimović, Dejan Pejaković, Josip Pejaković, Saša Pejaković, Vesna Mašić, Damir Nikšić, Lejla Graho, Selma Učanbarlić, Osman Proho, Aida Hajduković Kristiansen, Farah Kristiansen, Thomas Kristiansen, Bakir Karić, Braco Dimitrijević, Elma Međedović, Kalid Spahić, Maja Bajević, Mersida Bučan, Edin Arifhodžić, Denis Ilić, Denis Demša, Lejla Demša, Dennis Gratz, Dževad Karahasan, Adnan Ćuhara, Žan Marolt, Tatjana Šojić, Olga Kurylenko, Sabina Bambur, Alex Elena, Sanin Hašimbegović, Dino Bajrović, Asja Čengić, Almir Imširević, Hanan Imširević, Aldin Imširević, Louis Fortier, Boris Šiber, Ridley Scott, Sabit Sejdinović, Danijela Stanić Sejdinović, Elena Sejdinović, Mona Sejdinović, Zenit Đozić, Saida Fišeković, Fernando Leon de Aranoa, Vladan Petković, Boban Skerlić, Aleksandar Jevđević, Srđan Jevđević, Luc Besson, Branko Đurić, Tanja Ribič, Zala Đurić Ribić, Damir Arslanagić, Mirsad Kličić, Lana Milašinović, Naida Pinjo Džigal, Lamija Pinjo Džigal, Fedža Milavić, Nataša Mirković, Izudin Bajrović, Senad Bašić, Jasna Bašić Pozder, Mladen Popović, Alen Kurtović, Alen Schmidt, Emir Zametica, Nina Đogo Gracić, Selma Spahić, Bojan Hadžihalilović, Darko Došlo, Dragomir Križić, Mladen Jeličić, Nirvana Žiško, Igor Musulin, Haris Žiško, Sanida Žiško, Belma Žiško, Nadine Mičić, Zara Čengić, Tara Thaller, Elvir Rašić, Ado Šahbaz, Kristian Budak, Igor Kučinović, Amel Đikoli, Jasmina Đikoli, Almir Đikoli, Anthony Dod Mantle, Zoran Ćatić, Lejla Omeragić

Ćatić, Dario Šimić, Mario Šimić, Max von Sidov, Alex Dickson, Jusuf Hadžifejzović, Marcela Valerio Guimaraes, Ante Benić, Ivuša Benić, Adnan Hajrulahović, Kenan Tuzi, Lucija Kelava, Adi Vejzagić, Ervina Muftić, Muhamed Karamehmedović, Ensar Halilović, Lara Halilović, Rada Švrakić, Ismir Jusko, Anđela Kusić, Nešo Kovač, Enes Zlatar, Admir Dželmo, Ervin Nevesinjac, Damir Nevesinjac, Mirela Lambić, Milutin Kusmuk, Alen Halak, Antonela Pehar Šimunović, Mehmed Porča, Adnan Hadžić, Altijana Marić Đorđević, Sanel Marić, Edin Ahmetović, Nataša Hajdarević, Kenan Kulenović, Duško Bugarin, Mirsad Herović, Gordana Boban, Terrence Malick, Lidija Lejla Kordić, Sead Karkelja, Jelena Jovanova, Jana Stojanovska, Tom Hardy, Viktor Kljajić, Ana Tikvić, Saša Petrović, Nancy Ownalla Abdalla Abdel Sakhi, Daniel Craig, Marinko Prga, Nigel Casey, Mario Leko, Andrea Dugandžić, Emina Trumić, Sanja Cvijanović, Dea Kisi, Almir Čengić, Safet Rašinlić, Adnan Branković, Azra Silajdžić, Goran Trkulja, Feđa Nikolinović, Slaven Španović, Goran Grgić, Nusret Pašić, Aida Alilović Jokanović, Irfan Ribić, Irfan Redžović, Nirman Moranjak Bamburać, Dragan Jovičić, Caroline Ferguson, Edward Ferguson, Samir Omeradžić, Mustafa Čebo, Atena Stegert, Pero Desnica, Selma Ramić, Antonio Franić, Milivoj Beader, Jadranka Đokić, Marija Simonović, Nataša Petrovic, Admir Šabić, Zehra Kreho, Aida Bukva, Boro Đukanović, Jasna Diklić, Bogdan Diklić, Pjer Žalica, Jasna Žalica, Ismar Žalica, Antonije Žalica, Luna Zimić Mijović, Nataša Petrović, Haris Memija, Kemal Čebo, Olja Runjić, Belma Lizde Kurt, Aleš Kurt, Mirza Salković, Emir Fejzić, Milutin Petrović, Amra Bakšić Čamo, Igor Čamo, Amar Jugo, Nataša Kršulj, Stjepan Voženilek, Senad Hadžifejzović, Mirza Hadžibegović, Adis Tanović, Oliver Barišić, Ida Sefić, Ena Vatrić Bubica, Nedim Bubica, Emina Huko, Belma Lalić, Zulfikar Filandra, Nemanja Goronja, Stefan Karanović, Alen Crnalić, Zlatan Crnalić, Sara Crnalić Savić, Tanja Crnalić, Rade Čajić, Deni Mešić, Rade Jungić, Boban Prodanović, Božo Vrećo, Selma Gaši, Zoran Dragičević, Dino Šaran, Adnan Šaran, Srđan Vuletić, Sanela Hodžić, Alma Ferović Fazlić, Staša Dukić, Miško Czerkas,

Helena Vuković, Arnan Hukanović, Dino Hukanović, Daniel Hukanović, Selma Hukanović, Chris Dale, Archie Dale, Joe Shooman, Mirvad Zenuni, Edina Kasumagić, Tanja Đurović, Katja Bratković, Aida Amin El Hadari Pediša, Damir Pediša, Ina Malkoč, Maja Čengić, Tanja Miletić Oručević, Filip Gajić, Minja Huseinović, Drago Buka, Sam Mendes, Amila Terzi- mehić, Ashley Judd, Nihad Kreševljaković, Sead Kreševlja- ković, Hamdija Kreševljaković, Darko Janjić, Murat Abdiho- džić, Alen Podgorica, Nataša Vicić, Almas Smajlović, Belma Salkunić, Sean Bean, Ivana Perkunić Mešalić, Adnan Mešalić, Ika Ferrer Gotić, Goran Popara, Tanja Mandić Popara, Minela Jašar Opardija, Hana Popaja, Rijad Smajović, Indy, Amila Ramović, Tijana Cvjetićanin, Dejan Kajević, Dunja Galineo Kajević, Remy Ourdan, Srđan Kurpjel, Siniša Udo- vičić, Zlatko Hadžidedić, Željko Živković, Nada Đurevska, Dženita Imamović Omerović, Milan Dević, Katarina Stij- čević, Maglen Stipčević, Thomas Vinterberg, Leonardo Šarić, Ivan Šarić, Tarik Džinić, Bojan Miholjčić, Muhamed Dželi- lović, Mersad Čuljević, Lejla Jusić, Aleksandra Savić, Marija Karan, Edin Zubčević, Darko Perić, Admir Švrakić, Aleksan- dra Vujović, Alen Ekmečić, Tonči Marinić, Goran Zorić, Mak Čengić, Sara Ažman, Ana Babić, Dragan Nikolić, Alisa Šišić Babichev, Faruk Šehić, Miša Stančev, Lana Stanišić, Rijad Vojniković, Tarik Samarah, Alban Ukaj, Berna Balić, Bernarda Tolić, Goran Udovičić, Aida Lopčalija, Emir Lop- čalija, Edin Lopčalija, Ines Lopčalija, Maša Hilčišin, Maya Petrovna, Sergej Vujanović, Faruk Halilović, Elvir Laković, Robert Pečnik, Almir Manjo, Maja Drnda, Aida Čorbadžić, Nikola Inđić, Dragan Inđić, Dragan Inđić, Milan Inđić, Lidija Opačić, Martina Saira Keškić, Ljubica Ostojić, Mak Hubjer, Amina Malagić, Berina Malagić, Jack Dimich, Admir Lasić, Amir Voloder, Dragana Poznić, Hamzalija Bošnjak, Nađa Čengić, Danijela Vinš, Nina Violić, Enis Hrnjić, Haris Ho- džić, Mirza Hurem, Naida Đekić, Nermin Žiga, Adnan Pezo, Edo Vejselović, Emela Burdžović, Azra Širovnik, Barbara Hatta Širovnik, Asja Moškon Širovnik, Mediha Musliović, Anderson Cooper, Tomislav Cvitanušić, Igor Valka, Goran Valka, Srđan Valka, Milka Valka, Petar Valka, Aleksandar

Seksan, Danko Kukić, Jasenko Pašić, Boris Ler, Mirna Ler, Davor Sabo, Melita Šišić, Alma Hadžić, Dina Hajdarević, Lejla Hodžić, Edin Hajdarević, Dino Bajraktarević, Antonije Pušić, Elvir Muminović, Elvira Muminović, Vesna Andre Zaimović, Dragan Rokvić, Ognjenka Rokvić, Elvira Judenić, Miško Judenić, Ena Judenić, Dalal Midhat, Tijana Dapčević, Ćazim Dervišević, Damir Begović, Vanesa Glođo, Svjetlana Andrić, Tarik Učanbarlić, Nermin Džombić, Iman Džombić, Adem Jež, Amir Zlatar, Tarik Jusufbašić, Izudin Kolečić, Milan Pavlović, Semir Krivić, Baisa Krivić, Darko Jelisić, Muhamed Tepić, Narcis Tepić, Emina Ganić, Miralem Zup-čević, Adnan Kreso, Zoran Ivančić, Sergej Trifunović, Branislav Trifunović, Admir Glamočak, Tim Robbins, Dragan Marinković, Mustafa Behmen, Almir Domanagić, Damir Kustura, Srđan Šarenac, Šemsudin Maljević, Emir Herenda, Martina Mlinarević, Duška Bilbija Tabori, Duško Filipan, Mika Filipan, Mirela Filipan Čeklić, Timka Grin, Gail Stevens, Adi Jež, Nancy Bishop, Danis Tanović, Ben Kingsley, Davor Golubović, Melanie Thierry, Anila Gajević, Edin Avdagić, Buba Gavrankapetanović, Mirza Dervišić, Benicio del Toro, Ana Kobelja, Almir Panjeta, Dragan Bursać, Lamija Hadžihasanović Homarac, Benjamin Čengić, Elizabeta Sotele, Adnan Salihagić, Emir Dukatar, Rasim Jusufović, Selma Poljaković Jusufović, Dalibor Matanić, Helena Minić Matanić, Fatima Kazazić Obad, Donald Sutherland, Adnan Omeović, Safeta Varagić, Šahin Šišić, Senad Hasanović, Bojana Škrobić Omerović, Eldin Nuhić, Nermin Čengić, Belma Alić, Lejla Alić, Jasmin Duraković, Kemal Alečković, Esad Brkić, Elmir Jukić, Mona Muratović, Selma Štrbo, Anita Kajasa Memović, Samra Mlinar Mandić, Mirsad Tuka, Jasenka Kratović, Fikret Kadrić, Ana Marija Grubač, Admir Avdić, Mina Salkić, Selma Dizdar, Mirela Trepanić, Redžinald Šimek, Mirza Musa, Ayani Musa, Edhem Husić, Miraj Grbić, Marija Omaljev Grbić, Selma Alispahić, Selma Berisalić, Marko Kovačević, Dino Delić, Edin Ramulić, Azer Guzin, Semjuel Dedić, Jasmin Šehović, Tanja Smoje, Dina Selimović, Gaša Miladinović, Mladen Vitomir, Suada Ahmetašević, Mirza Tanović, Damir Uzunović, Ines Tanović, Lazar Dragoević, Lejla Pajić,

Kerim Čutuna, Nedim Mujić, Adis Tiro, Tanja Dijak Tiro, Vanja Matović, Maja Avdibegović, Mirza Muzurović, Nataša Govedarica, Nedim Alikadić, Una Bejtović, Emina Kujundžić, Stjepan Roš, Tatjana Roš, Vanja Lisac, Jan Kulenović, Džana Pinjo, Dalibor Tanić, Beatrice Kruger, Alma Mulahasanović Klier, Sadžida Šetić, Edvin Šimić, Mladen Relić, Marija Šuković, Atila Filipovitz, Nikola Musa, Antonio Musa, Mario Drmać, Alisa Čajić Drmać, Ivana Stojadinović, Adis Đapo, Ivana Vojinović, Pavica Pogarčić, Faris Pinjo, Admir Crvčanin, Nedžad Hrnjica, Maja Kljakić Hrnjica, Dragan Tanić, Sanja Tanić, Danijela Dugandžić, Una Mujadžić, Tarik Helić, Zlatan Omerović, Nedžad Begović, Sabrina Begović Ćorić, Vesna Milek, Amina Begović, Aida Smailhodžić Hadžić, Amila Hadžić, Ado Hadžić, Danijela Knežević, Miroslav Vidojević, Petar Lončar, Nenad Mandić, Rada Mandić, Jasenko Odžaković, Kristina Ljevak, Adis Billain Kutkut, Trevor Gibson, Atila Šalaka, Emir Jugo, Boban Pejičić, Miodrag Trifunov, Adnan Lugonić, Sabina Šabić, Damir Kurtagić, Nenad Kovačević, Stefan Pejović, Edib Ahmetašević, Vanja Pavlović, Mario Knezović, Muhamed Muminović, Simona Ličen, Aleksandar Hemon, Mirza Požega, Ema Šeremet, Faris Avdić, Osman Arslanagić, Amela Vilić, Marinko Nikolić, Omar Mehmedbašić, Jasmin Vila, Armin Hadžić, Fikret Mujkić, Igor Sabljić, Ahmed Likić, Emir Akvić, Mirvad Kurić, Almir Kurt, Senka Kurt, Sin Kurt, Zlatan Muslić, Elma Juković, Nada Zečević, Maja Zećo, Tea Pokrajčić, Aldin Omerović, Bruce Dickinson, Andrea Aković, Dino Bajramović, Aleksandra Balmazović, Merima Lepić, Željko Škarić, Vlado Čubak, Jasmina Čubak, Darija Lorenci, Andrej Kostanjevec, Tarik Karačić, Jelena Kordić, Tea Šimić, Haris Alić, Mejra Makaš, Haris Pašović, Vlado Cabrera, Nikola Đuričko, Ljiljana Đuričko, Rikardo Druškić, Naomi Druškić, Damir Šeremet, Mirjana Hrga, Đani Pervan, Pablo Huetos, Igor Baroš, Veronica Jacob, Alen Kaikčija, Lajla Kaikčija, Rade Jagličić, Moamer Kasumović, Nina Hadžić, Malka Turkušić, Edin Mehić, Sejdalija Kutlovac, Izet Kutlovac, Safet Kutlovac, Aziz Arnautović, Rea Jugo, Saša Peševski, Marina Matić, Negra Bradić, Mirna Kreso, Alen Muratović, Danijela

Mijatović, Samir Hodović, Aldin Hodović, Ensar Sulejma-
nagić, Dejan Miholjčić, Tihana Lazović, Dejana Ždrakić,
Boško Ždrakić, Davor Pušić, Ivana Petrović, Edin Osmić,
Nadia Cvitanović, Sema Tataragić, Vedran Hrustanović,
Kemal Rizvanović, Enisa Njemčević, Bakir Njemčević, Almin
Zrno, Hana Zrno, Emina Muftić, Admir Šehović, Adisa
Vrabac, Adnan Beširović, Aleksandar Hršum, Amela Kalabić,
Damir Ramović, Srđan Radanović, Mimo Šahinpašić, Dino
Sarija, Senad Alihodžić, Igor Skvarica, Toby Spigel, Tihomir
Stanić, Ismar Volić, Brian Kelley, Slaven Vidak, Saša Handžić,
Dragan Komadina, Asja Krsmanović, Saša Krmpotić, Filip
Radovanović, Amir Bjelanović, Amar Ćustović, Samir Baj-
raktarević, Darija Badnjević, Svjetlana Brezo, Faruk Lonča-
rević, Christiane Amanpour, Amra Kapidžić, Merima Ovči-
na, Selma Rustempašić, Adriana Domazet, Senad Ljuca,
Biljana Bijeljanin Vučinić, Belma Buljubašić, Mina Bašić,
Sanjin Arnautović, Lela Laković, Emina Tulić, Nermin Tulić,
Sloven Anzulović, Predrag Doder, Ramiz Huremagić, Ali
Adnan Grahić, Sandy Lopičić, Gordana Magaš, Elma Ahme-
tović, Ištvan Gabor, Srđan Puhalo, Mugdim Avdić, Irfan
Habibović, Nino Berbić, Jasminka Beri, Darjan Bilić, Dževad
Pejdah, Faris Arapović, Igor Mulamuhić, Irena Mulamuhić,
Dunja Tatomirović, Ena Bojičić, Aleksandra Kostić, Alem
Babić, Otac Hrizostom, Sulejman Bugari, Davor Ebner, Rijad
Gvozden, Sanin Čepalo, Marc Kohen, Nidžara Ahmetašević,
Rade Čolović, Cristobal Krusen, Enis Bešlagić, Darko Brkan,
Boris Brkan, Laurence Jackson, Aida Bećirović, Vanda Kljajo,
Slađana Jaha, Džanan Jaha, Miro Purivatra, Patricio Corona,
Selma Omerović, Siniša Holik, Manja Huzbašić, Hana
Bajrović, Debbie McWilliams, Rezak Hukanović, Abdulah
Sidran, Sanja Dervišević, Sanela Krsmanović Bistrivoda,
Mirza Šahović, Ena Kurtalić, Vila Sutović, Eldin Sutović, Lara
Sutović, Rea Sutović, Džejla Glavović, Istok Bratić, Nedfeim
Lipa, Sandra Ozimica, Damir Smajić, Tanja Smajić, Ena Sma-
jić, Emina Hodžić Adilović, Biljana Semiz, Faruk Mulaome-
rović, Elma Islamović, Nedžad Podžić, Colin Firth, Teta
Sena, Erol Zubčević, Ahmed Burić, Vesna Hadžiosmanović,
Ado Šatara, Almir Žunić, Haris Vlahovljak, Orhan Maslo,

Vanja Nogo, Boris Lalić, Frank Feys, Tijana Ognjanović, Belmina Ibrišević, Berina Hamidović, Vladimir Kajević, Ivica Pinjuh, Alma Merunka, Sanja Golubović Samardžić, Dean Golubović, Boris Popović, Adis Čingić, Samir Plasto, Jadran Crnogorac, Danijela Gogić, Samir Mehić, Ejla Bavčić, Ermin Sijamija, Tea Feriz, Peđa Bajović, Naida Kundurović, Igor Vranić, Ajla Frljučkić Cabrera, Dejan Ostojić, Nemanja Lazić, Miloš Timotijević, Hiba Begić, Nevzeta Musabegović, Dina Mušanović, Senad Bešić, Mato Barišić, Lana Bašić, Elma Tataragić, Alen Drljević, Miloš Janković, Amela Kapeta-nović, Dinka Imamović Trako, Muharem Trako, Armin Trako, Nermin Trako, Nebojša Glogovac, Rada Kraišnik, Igor Kraišnik, Blanka Kraišnik, Jasmin Đorđević, Adela Alagić Đorđević, Dea Đorđević, Lena Đorđević, Šemsudin Gegić, Emina Gegić, Vedrana Drljepan, Igor Drljača, Sanja Burić, Faruk Šabanović, Nikolina Vujić, Meliha Ćilimković, Enis Voloder, Lejla Čehajić, Loris Gutić, Ivana Đurić, Arma Tano-vić, Christopher Peditto, Vildana Drljević, Haris Drljević, Branislav Lečić, Armin Nesiren, Alen Šimić, Saša Stanar, Sanja Zijadić Bećirević, Luna Kalaš, Dženana Kalaš, Maja Salkić, Dušan Vranić, Amel Tahirović, Ediba Bakira Trbonja Kapić, Anja Drljević, Aldin Tucić, Šerif Aljić, Nadža Pušilo, Ermin Bravo, Amira Lekić, Jasmila Žbanić, ElviraAlišahović Gelo, Holly Goline, Fahrudin Kreštalica, Nebojša Šerić, Nusmir Muharemović, Mugdim Avdagić, Faketa Salihbegović Avdagić, Mustafa Mustafić, Alena Džebo, Nikola Kojo, Zijah Gafić, Damir Mujagić, Saša Lošić, Jordi van Even, Tea Temim, Damir Imamović, Dino Mustafić, Elvedina Sultanović, Zlatan Školjić, Lejla Panjeta, Almir Bašić, Verica Sabranović, Amel Baftić, Edna Fainaru, Dan Fainaru, Nisrin Kršlak, Sanja Džeba, Mirna Duhaček, Satko Mujagić, Simona Maksimović, Slobodan Maksimović, Almir Kenović, Zoran Mlinarević, Darko Lukić, Ivona Baković, Enes Kozličić, Jovan Marjanović, Edin Ramović, Robert Krajinović, Milorad Kapor, Dado Čaušević, Dino Šukalo, Erol Bihorac, Zvijezdana Žepčanin, Mavrak Matea, Riad Avdić, Harun Ćehović, Davor Domazet, Ena Husić, Ina Arnautalić, Snežana Vidović, Lana Zablocki, Nermin Hamzagić, Ademir Kenović, Selma Kenović, Lana

Delić, Enes Salković, Uranela Agić Burina, Haris Burina, Kerim Mašović, Zlata Zubović, Tea Zubović, Atila Šukalo, Zlatan Šukalo, Nedim Džinović, Jasmin Geljo, Nenad Đurić, Hatidža Nuhić, Mirsad Džombić, Damir Šagolj, Jasmin Ferović, Mirza Đugum, Emir Kapetanović, Tijana Vignjević, Mario Katavić, Željka Katavić Pilj, Belma Jusufović, Ilda Oswald, Sanel Agić, Sanela Agić, Meldin Hota, Alen Ajanović, Feđa Isović, Emir Hasanović, Jasmin Salčin, Ejub Kučuk, Amina Kučuk, Goran Stanković, Snežana van Houwelingen, Wouter van Houwelingen, Nedžad Mulaomerović, Dario Novalić, Esad Bratović, Branko Vrdoljak, Samir Pašalić, Milomir Kovačević, Martin Morris, Tarik Filipović, Aida Begić, Romina Vitasović, Nedeljko Čalija, Željko Josip Topalović, Zina Čengić, Mona Čengić, Edis Bilić, Maja Jurić, Dušan Joksimović, Almir Palata, Amina Huseinčehajić, Željko Božić, Milkica Božić, Senka Baralić, Edin Hadžagić, Ivana Dragičević, Tim Clancy, Admir Šarkić, Almin Hrustemović, Goran Kostić, Ivan Ramadan, Jim Marshall, Goran Navojec, Bojan Trišić, Davor Tadić, Nedim Zlatar, Haris Kuljuh, Elvir Alihodžić, Nenad Nurudinović, Mirza Sijerčić, Emin Voloder, Nihad Zečević, Mustafa Ljajić, Sena Ljajić, Alija Ljajić, Zana Marjanović, Mirna Dizdarević, Dino Rogić, Ida Keškić, Milan Sokolović, Mirza Ćorić, Momo Lađević, Darko Ostojić, Damir Karakaš, Muhamed Hadžović, Vedrana Božinović, Irfan Avdić, Almir Čehajić, Damir Krčum, Dajana Zilić, Oliver Dujmović, Andrej Hamzić, Stefano Giantin, Ana Kuzmanović, Alma Talibećirević, Mirza Halilović, Tinka Milinović, Davor Janjić, Zlatko Suhonić, Mehmed Ratkušić, Zulejha Kečo, Jovana Milosavljević, Jasenko Matković, Adnan Đindo, Jelena Paunović, Jelena Milušić, Mirsad Ćatić, Goran Esapović, Mehmed Kekić, Mirsad Kekić, Erol Gagula, Segor Hadžagić, Nerman Mahmutović, Jasmin Ališpago, Darko Poljak, Nermin Puškar, Denis Švrakić, Gea Erjavec, Adnan Hasković, Faris Dobrača, Irma Alimanović, Katarina Nikšić, Riad Ljutović, Aleksandar Dimitrijević, Nedim Nezirović, Jasmin Mehić, Mila Gabriela Tabori, Lana Sinanović Ramljak, Dejan Bućin, Ema Gežo, Maksim Jelavić, Nermin Lagumdžija, Gabor Tabori, Paula Farias, Amela Mehić, Marija Stošić, Nebojša

Šavija Valha, Ognjen Šavija, Zlatko Ganić, Džemil Ličina, Tanja Radišić, Dubravka Bušatlija, Tatjana Ždiara, Faruk Borić, Mirela Milak, Nermin Karačić, Elameri Škrgić, Hasija Borić Stojić, Jovana Golubović, Samra Tojaga, Samra Jahić, Karla Matošić, Petar Miličević, Miralem Musabegović, Nataša Savić, Ado Hasanović, Ranko Tica, Ismet Arnautalić, Lejla Karišik, Nataša Kučera, Darko Kalaš, Darko Ler, Muharem Vojniković, Orijana Kunčić, Lana Barić, Dario Raos, Edin Zorlak, Dženana Musemić, Koštana Džinić Mulovi, Semir Afan Muzurović, Branko Lustig, Pierre Spengler, Ammara Mistrić, Fuad Backović, Affan Žiško, Maša Čampara Fejzić, Emir Hadžihafizbegović, Aida Hadžihafizbegović, Edin Hadžihafizbegović, Amra Hadžihafizbegović, Almir Bašović, Asmir Kujović, Sarah Krusen, Adin Fejzić, Mirza Mutevelić, Ermin Mujezinović, Bakir Hadžiomerović, Nikola Kuridža, Selma Kafedžić, Leila Jahić, Naila Jahić, Mirza Mušija, Sabiha Alibašić, Lana Marlović, Hamza Ražnatović, Oljeg Ražnatović, Lejla Balić, Tatjana Vuković Požega, Muamer Bečić, Suvad Kičević, Aida Mulahusejnović, Sandra Behramović, Elma Čomor, Boris Pušić, Sretko Vujić, Jasmin Rahmanović, Sulejman Kadić, Valentin Inzko, Danilo Kreso, Maid Dedić, Nedžad Mulahusejnović, Ljubinka Klarić, Vanja Pušić, Vedran Đekić, Dario Bevanda, Bojana Vidosavljević, Vedran Fajković, Suad Mujkanović, Edib Hadžić, Lenka Šerbedžija, Ismir Omeragić, Valentina Gumhold, Duška Gavrilović, Gaša Gavrilović, Nikita Gavrilović, Boris Gavrilović, Sead Seković, Nina Šikić, Željko Šikić, Anita Šikić, Denis Šikić, Maja Izetbegović, Olivera Petrović, Zulfikar Ališpago, Elvira Tica, Feđa Tica, Anja Tica, Duško Grmuša, Nikola Šerbedžija, Beka Šerbedžija, Vojin Šerbedžija, Borko Šerbedžija, Vanja Nikolinović, Siniša Čomora, Amra Dukatar, Anja Tomić, Renata Ponjević, Dado Džihan, Narcis Babić, Saša Oručević, Marija Kovačić Šmalcelj, Nikola Indić, Lidija Opačić, Mirza Hajrić, Snežana van Houwelingen, Wouter van Houwelingen, Dragan Bjelogrlić, Esma Numanović, Muhamed Tepić, Narcis Tepić, Cheryl Krusen, Jasmina Izetbegović, Sanjin Draganović, Antonije Pušić, Damir Marjanović, Midhat Kapo, Boriša Gavrilović, Edin Pobrić, Aleksandar Trifunović.

CIP - Katalogizacija u publikaciji
Nacionalna i univerzitetska biblioteka
Bosne i Hercegovine, Sarajevo

821.163.4(497.6)-31

ŠTUKAN, Feđa
    Blank / Feđa Štukan ; [translated from Bosnian by Ediba-
Bakira Trbonja-Kapić]. - Sarajevo : autor, 2020. - 232 str. ; 20 cm

Bilješke uz tekst.

ISBN 978-9926-484-06-4

COBISS.BH-ID 41202438